Radio control in model boats

Radio control in model boats

All about ships, boats and yachts

John Cundell

Argus Books

Argus Books
Argus House
Boundary Way
Hemel Hempstead
Herts HP2 7ST
England

Reprinted 1987
2nd edition 1989
Reprinted 1991

ISBN 1 85486 002 X

Phototypesetting by Photocomp Ltd., Birmingham

Printed and bound by BPCC Wheatons Ltd, Exeter

Contents

1 / Wavelengths

Radio is no longer the mystery it was to our forefathers: indeed it is probably fair to say that only a very small proportion of the world's population have never used or heard a radio receiver in operation. Most people, even the most primitive, seem to accept without question the fact that they can listen to a voice or music from the other side of the world or even from another world such as the moon, yet they seem absolutely amazed that a model can be commanded to move in a precise and defined manner by an operator wielding a transmitter quite close to the model – usually well within visual range of the user as well.

There is really no more mystery or magic with radio control operation than there is with conventional broadcasting. In fact in many respects the requirements are much less exacting. The physical elements involved are very similar, the difference being that the signal sent by a remote control transmitter is really just a set of electrical signals which will be decoded by the receiver and made to operate electronic or mechanical switches which in turn operate devices known as servo mechanics. These latter units can then be arranged to move rudders or speed up and slow down electric motors or switch on lights, etc., i.e. remotely control the model in such a way that the unknowing watcher believes that a human operator is in command.

The first radio control boat

There is a recorded example of radio control as early as the beginning of this century. In 1905 a Professor Branly demonstrated remote operation of machinery for an industrial requirement and in the early 1920s a model airship was supposedly controlled by radio during a music hall performance.

There is some disagreement as to the first recorded occurrences of radio control being used to control a boat, whether it be model or full-size. There is a documented case though at Lake Windermere in Cumbria as far back as 1920. Radio control experiments took place at the north end of the lake with the recently restored full-size powerboat

The full-size Windermere Steam Launch *Bat* was one of the first boats to be controlled by radio. This exhibition-standard model is also radio controlled and further detailed photographs of the installation will be found in other chapters.

White Lady, now on permanent display at the Windermere Steamboat Museum at Bowness. Unfortunately none of the radio control apparatus still exists. It must be assumed that the system was that known as spark generated. An electrical spark releases a surge of energy into the ether, causing a short radio emission over a wide band of frequencies. It is fairly simple to detect this emission and for the receiving apparatus to switch a circuit. Spark equipment is not used at all today as it is extremely dirty, speaking electrically, and causes severe interference over the entire radio spectrum.

Interest in radio control for models started in the 1930s in the United States of America, mainly for the emerging hobby of model aircraft which was undergoing dramatic expansion due to the introduction of mass-produced model spark ignition engines.

There was little development, if any, in the model boating world, either in the United States or in Great Britain. The use of radio control was restricted to the Forces, who made use of the apparatus for controlling unmanned target ships and aircraft. Modellers with a maritime interest were presumably quite happy with straight running models, functional and scale, and for the speed enthusiast models were run tethered around a pole. Both these forms of model boating have stayed with us to the present day and indeed have recently been undergoing a new lease of life. However, in comparison with the numbers now enjoying radio control the percentages are very small. But we are jumping ahead of our story.

The second world war years created further interest in technology, yet during the late 1940s and into the early '50s modelling was still very much the province of the model engineer. There were virtually no commercial components available for model boat use and only limited material for aircraft modellers. However, with the advent of the small diesel in the late '40s, a number of manufacturers realised the potential of model boating and began converting the engines for maritime use and producing a limited range of fittings. Some of the names are still

An advertisement in Model Maker magazine which appeared in 1964 detailing crude R/C gear and the first range of commercial boat fittings and hardware. Ripmax are still with us today as one of the UK's major model distributors.

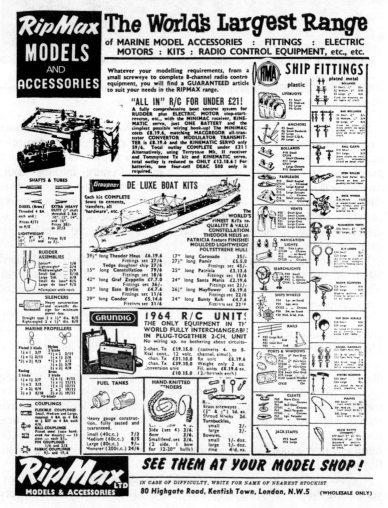

round today, for instance Ripmax and Hales, to name just two. Is it a coincidence or fate that Ripmax are today the British distributors of the best known range of radio control equipment available throughout the world, namely Futaba?

Early radio control events

According to our records one of the first ever radio control model boat events was at Blackpool in August 1952. The competition was divided up into three sections, for boats equipped with rudder control only, operated by escapement, the more advanced power boats and radio control yachts. The escapement boats included a number of the *Wavemaster* launch which was one of the first commercially advertised models, selling in January 1953 for £3.65.

At the Poole club's radio event in September, one of the entrants was to become the leading designer for many years in the UK of radio control equipment, and the name behind the first really successful British radio control equipment manufacturer, namely one George Honnest-Redlich.

George Honnest-Redlich was a pioneer of radio control and made the first crossing of the English Channel with a radio controlled model in 1951. Here the model is undergoing tests on the Thames before the crossing. (Photo courtesy Kevin Desmond).

George had already made quite a name for himself in 1951 when his 3.46cc powered launch, *Miss ED*, named after the firm Electronic Developments, made the first crossing of the Channel under radio control from an accompanying chase boat. The radio was a three function tuned reed outfit, which we will describe in a little more detail later.

Reports of these events were carried in the major hobby magazine of the time, *Model Maker*, which started life in 1950, taking over from *Model Mechanics*. This magazine at last gave manufacturers a vehicle to advertise their wares and although the magazine catered for all forms of modelling, it rapidly became very marine oriented, until in 1965 it changed its title to *Model Boats* and for many years was the only regular model boating monthly. The amount of material on radio control had grown regularly, until late in 1985 when it was impossible to cater for all forms of the model boating hobby within one monthly title, hence *Radio Control Boat Modeller* was launched as a bimonthly magazine.

Early equipment

Early commercial radio control equipment was bulky, to say the least. The transmitter was a large metal box about 1ft cube and stood on the ground. Its large size was not only due to the relatively large size of the components, i.e. valves etc., but mainly due to the hefty 120 volt dry battery required to power the valves. A smaller low voltage battery was also needed. A tall 8ft aerial from aluminium tubes which slotted into one another (and which doubled as superb boat recovering devices until they inadvertently got dropped into the water, the reason why practically all transmitters sported 2ft tall aerials!) radiated the signals. Control was effected by a small hand held box connected to the receiver by a wire. The box contained a button which when pushed made a circuit and resulted in a continuous carrier wave being transmitted by the ground based transmitter. The receiver was about 4in by 4in with a tall valve and also required a high voltage to work, usually around 45 volts with a 1.5 volt low voltage battery as well. The receiver drew a relatively high current when in the waiting mode – that was with the transmitter inactive or not keyed – however, when the carrier wave was sent on pressing the transmit button, the receiver current fell to a relatively low value. This value could be detected and used to operate a relay which itself could be used to switch an actuator or mechanical mechanism. It was soon realised that the system would work much better if the transmitter was sending all the time and interrupted by the button, so holding the receiver in its low current condition most of the time except when keyed. The system was difficult to set up and the relay operation was extremely sensitive as the current changes involved were very small. Reliability was improved with the advent of better circuitry and amplification, but it was the introduction of the tone system which enabled the next major breakthrough.

Tone

A low frequency audio or tone signal was superimposed on the carrier, which was on all the time, and the tone only sent on signalling (pushing the button). The receiver circuit was designed to have a minimal operating current with no signal which fell low on receipt of the carrier wave, and which rose to a steady maximum on detection of the tone.

The tone was sent at approximately 800 cycles per second. As receivers became more sensitive, it was realised that if they could detect different tonal frequencies, perhaps more than one operation could be carried out. This led to what became to be called multi-channel working. The transmitter would contain a number of separate tone generators and a corresponding number of buttons, each of which could switch on one of the tone generators and modulate the carrier signal accordingly. The receiver is tuned to the carrier wave frequency but additionally needs extra circuitry to differentiate between the changing tones. This could be done electronically but in practice was found impractical over three channels, although a number of German manufacturers persevered for many years with up to six channel systems.

The system which soon gained universal acceptance and which was extremely reliable in its day utilised a reed bank. We have already mentioned this development when we spoke about George Honnest-Redlich's crossing of the Channel. Tones at different audio wavelengths were generated by the transmitter and sent out according to which button was pressed on the transmitter. The receiver didn't attempt to separate the tones electronically, but sent them to a bank of small metal reeds cut to different lengths. Like the tuning fork on a piano these would only vibrate at a certain frequency governed by their length. The reeds were allowed to vibrate against a minute contact and this electrical signal pulled in a relay. The equipment did not develop all that quickly and it was 1958 before six channel gear became commonly available. The cost of the three channel outfit in 1953 was £23.75 complete; in today's terms £200 plus.

Despite these improvements the number of users was still relatively small, mainly because the modeller was still required to carry out a considerable amount of installation work, in particular wiring the equipment into the model, and because only one set of equipment could be operated at one time. The type of circuit in use was called

Multi boat racing was all the rage in 1973. The boats were not as streamlined as today's designs but in basic concept have changed little. John Stidwill was representing Great Britain at a World Championships in South Africa. Below, an early radio Marblehead from an American kit in 1973; notice the lever arm sail control unit which was practically universal in the U.S.A. as opposed to winches in Britain. (Photo C. R. Jeffries).

super-regenerative and required all of the allocated waveband because of its poor sensitivity and selectivity. There was some improvement in speed of models from 10 to 20mph but models were still based upon full-size prototypes rather than being designed for a particular function such as speed or steering or racing.

Superhet arrives

Then in the early 1960s super-heterodyne was born. This was and is a much more selective circuit which is capable of operating on narrower frequency band widths and also with better reliability. But the most important breakthrough that this represented was the ability to operate more than one set of radio control equipment at one and the same time. There were events around 1960 where two boats could be raced together following careful tuning of super-regen gear, but the most exciting part of the day, the final between the two fastest boats left in the competition could not always be run because of radio interference. As soon as true multi radio equipment arrived, and was found to be reliable, really competitive racing of boats could take place.

Multi racing arrives

Initially the boats were traditional launch types with bigger and faster motors, including the American glow plug engine beginning to appear in great numbers and at reasonable prices. The excitement of multi racing, as it came to be called, attracted a new breed of competition-minded modeller who was interested in performance rather than tinkering with the radio. A corresponding new breed of boats was developed and new materials such as glass reinforced resin started to appear.

Multi racing developed rapidly in this country and in South Africa, mainly due to migrant Brits, but relatively slowly on the Continent. Most races were of 15 minutes duration which gradually extended to 30 minutes, which is still the norm, although there are now many one and even some two hour events. Boats typically race around an M shaped course of up to 220 yards in length. Today's multi race boats are unashamedly designed for the job in hand and employ every technique possible for maximum performance under wide conditions. Electric powered racing models have developed along similar lines to their internal combustion engined bigger brothers, although obviously the races are shorter.

But while the UK forged ahead on the multi boat front, we were rather left behind in most other categories and Great Britain received

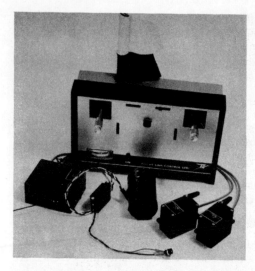

An early proportional superhet radio from a British manufacturer no longer in the business, Flight Link Control. The servos were unusual, using metal rather than plastic gears, which withstood knocks better. The transmitter case was also metal.

rather a rude awakening in 1967 when we sent our first team to the European Championships in Amiens and realised how far behind the rest of Europe we had fallen. Scale ships and boats were to a much higher standard than at home, except with one or two notable exceptions. However, the lessons were rapidly learned and we are now a force to be reckoned with in International competition on all fronts.

Radio had appeared in model yachts as early as 1950 but it was not really until 1970 onwards that things started moving. Perhaps model yachtsmen were less prepared than their power boat compatriots to dabble with things mechanical, but mainly of course, the yachtsman needs to be able to compete in the same race, like the multi man. In recent times the radio yacht has made great strides and has many advantages, not the least of which is no environmental problems.

Proportional control – the ultimate

We left the development of radio with the advent of superhet, but there was still one more significant invention to come in order for a radio controlled model to behave exactly as its full-size prototype – proportional control. This means the production of a control surface movement on the model which is exactly proportional to the amount of movement imparted to the transmitter stick. This demands a much more complex method of signalling and could only come about following the technological revolution which replaced the valve with the transistor.

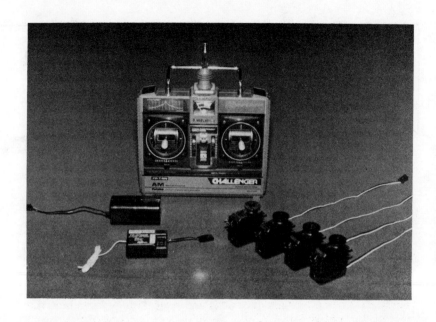

A typical modern 4-function outfit complete with four servos, dry cell battery pack, switch harness and receiver.

It was once thought, and stated often in the magazines of the period, that proportional control would never be achieved at a price which could be afforded by the average modeller, and certainly the first examples of the equipment were horrendously expensive. But large scale manufacture on an international basis, particularly by the Japanese, brought prices down to very acceptable standards by the mid seventies – even to one stage where a price war led to fully proportional two function equipment being sold for £12 complete. The industry has now settled down to producing extremely reliable price-conscious gear, or if the customer so desires, equipment so sophisticated that it will switch literally dozens of functions – very useful for scale demonstration models – or will actually include computer circuitry within the transmitter to remember often repeated or difficult combinations of commands. The reliability is at a standard which the pioneers of only 30 years ago would find hard to accept. Radio control equipment has come of age and is now treated as a tool or a means to an end rather than a tinkerer's delight. It is the object of this book to help you get the best possible service from this wonderful tool.

2 The system

As stated earlier radio control for model use operates on the same principles and elements as radio broadcasting. It requires a transmitter, which is today mostly hand-held, to broadcast the coded signals which are picked up by a receiver tuned to the transmitter's specific frequency. The broadcast receiver decodes the transmitted information into speech or music but the radio control receiver decodes the signal into electrical impulses which can be used by the electro-mechanical devices called servos to perform physical operations within the model. Let's take a closer look at the major components.

The transmitter

The transmitter comprises a closed metal, or more usually these days, plastic box containing the required electronics and batteries. They come in a variety of colours, shapes and sizes. The styling and ergonomics are very important as the transmitter is the part of the equipment most susceptible to sales appeal. A box is still the best general term and despite the styling all transmitters will include the following items.

Usually mounted on top is the aerial and sometimes the on-off switch. The aerial transmits the high frequency signal, whose field somewhat resembles the shape of a gigantic doughnut, and is usually telescopic and can sometimes be removed for storage. The range of the transmitted signal is upwards of two miles, but most operators lose visual contact orientation of the model at little more than 200 yards, so there is ample strength to spare.

Always on the front will be the controlling joysticks which are fitted to variable resistances inside the transmitter. By moving these sticks and consequently moving the resistances, varying electrical currents are fed into the electronic circuits and processed to ultimately operate the servos by a corresponding proportional amount of movement in the model. The number of sticks depends upon the number of operational channels or functions that the radio control system is designed to

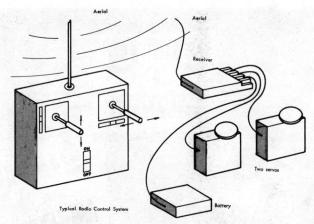

Typical Radio Control System

handle, but more on this subject later. Trims, small controls to enable one to adjust the neutral position of the related joystick and hence accurately 'centre' the corresponding servo are fixed adjacent to the joysticks.

An item again usually found on the front of the box is a battery voltage meter or radio frequency output meter to show that the transmitter is operating.

If the transmitter contains rechargeable batteries there will usually be a charging socket, sometimes underneath or otherwise at the rear, and perhaps a buddy box system for learners. The latter is in effect a

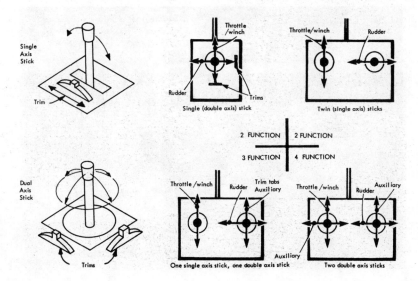

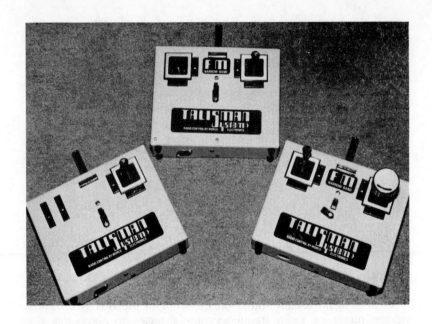

The Talisman can be ordered to suit individual requirements; from a British manufacturer, World Electronics. Shown are 2-function on one stick, 4-function on twin sticks and 5-function on one stick and a rotary stick which controls three functions. The 4-function outfit is shown complete below.

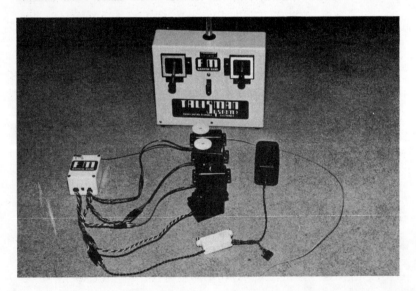

A computerised Pulse Code Modulation system which gives flexibility of control and practically eliminates interference is a feature of this modern 3-function outfit.

separate set of joysticks coupled to the main transmitter by a special cable which can be used by a learner to operate a model, but which can be totally overriden should difficulties arise by the tutor who retains control of the main transmitter unit. This system is more often used by aeromodellers rather than model boaters as accidents tend to be less terminal with water operation.

A most important although small access is the crystal socket. All except the very inexpensive outfits will have the capability of allowing you to choose the operating frequency within limits set by the Government and manufacturer. The crystal is a small and relatively delicate component manufactured to very close tolerances. A corresponding matching crystal fits into the receiver. We shall look at crystals in much more detail later. Many modellers tend to treat crystals badly. Don't. They can be jarred from their original setting and many problems arise, usually resulting in loss of control and sometimes interfering with other modellers' equipment.

The receiver

The receiver is a small box, again usually of plastic construction, measuring approximately 2.5in by 1.5in by 1in, although miniaturisation is resulting in much smaller units. These are of benefit for very small models or where weight is important as in some racing classes, but for the majority of applications the standard unit is completely acceptable. The case contains sockets to accept a power supply and connections to the servos, normally polarised to prevent incorrect

19

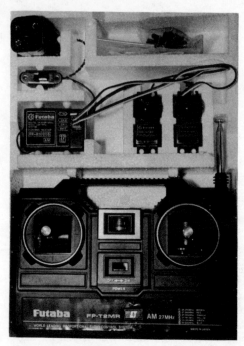

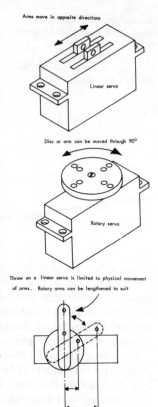

Arms move in opposite directions

Linear servo

Disc or arm can be moved through 90°

Rotary servo

Throw on a linear servo is limited to physical movement of arms. Rotary arms can be lengthened to suit

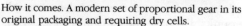

How it comes. A modern set of proportional gear in its original packaging and requiring dry cells.

connections, plus access to the receiver's crystal socket if a frequency change feature is incorporated. Finally the aerial wire consists of a length of wire approximately 18in long. The power supply harness usually includes an on/off switch ready wired by the manufacturer.

The servos

Servos are miniature electro-mechanical units about the size of a matchbox, each containing a small precision electric motor which drives an output shaft through an efficient gear train. The case is usually constructed from plastic, as are the gears, although some high power servos use metal gears. These are not needed for average use and the plastic type are quite capable of handling the forces generated from a rudder on a high performance power boat, for instance. The reduction ratio is about 1:20 which will develop several pounds of pull at the

20

servo arm. The latter can have a rotary to-and-fro movement of about 90 degrees or a linear movement along the servo.

When the servo receives a signal from the transmitter/receiver the motor turns, which rotates the servo output shaft via the gearbox. Attached to the output shaft within the servo case is a variable resistance. The electronic circuitry in the servo monitors the output from this resistance until the incoming signal is matched by the varying signal generated within the servo controlled by the resistance. When this state of affairs occurs, the motor stops. Hence if you move the joystick a small amount, the servo output arm will move a proportional amount – the over-riding reason as to why this method of control is known as proportional control.

Radio principles

Radio waves travel with the speed of light which is about 186000 miles per second, and they can be generated by any radio frequency (RF) current flowing in a circuit. RF is an alternating current as opposed to the direct current that flows from the battery when the circuit is made. The frequency is the number of complete waves generated in one second and is known as cycles/second or Hertz (Hz). These waves are generated at very high frequencies, ranging from approximately 1500Hz up to 100,000,000Hz. To remove the handling of large numbers, abbreviations are used, kilo or k for 1000 and mega or M for 1,000,000. Hence the spread above would be 1.5KHz to 100MHz.

Various parts of the radio spectrum, and that includes television which is simply a complicated radio signal, are assigned by the governing authorities, in the case of Great Britain by the Department of Trade and Industry, for various users. The part of the band given over for radio control users is restricted to different ranges in different countries. However, the almost universal range is 26.96 to 27.28MHz. Within the United Kingdom's allocated band it is possible to operate twelve different models at one and the same time on different frequencies or 'slots' as they are are known.

Although in America and some parts of Europe the band has suffered at the hands of Citizens' Band enthusiasts, particularly for model aircraft operation where interference is more liable and usually much more catastrophic than with a boat model, the authorities in this country, despite a period of chaos and confusion in the early unlicensed days of CB, have resisted infiltration on 27MHz AM, and CB channels are allocated part of the 27MHz FM band, on slightly different frequencies to those in general use by modellers. Experience has shown there is little if any interference caused to radio control users.

Most causes of control loss are not caused by interference, but nearly always by badly maintained or faulty equipment. There will always be those who operate illegal equipment, but if your radio gear is correctly aligned, relatively little if any trouble is to be experienced on 27MHz.

There are three other bands in Great Britain also allocated to radio control, 35MHz, 40MHz and 459MHz, the latter sometimes known as Ultra High Frequency (UHF). The former has been provided solely for model aircraft operation and this is a legal requirement. If your supplier tells you that 35MHz can be used in your area, he is inciting you to break the law. Because of this fact, your local club, being law abiding members of the National Association, will not allow the frequency to be used on their water.

Negotiations with the Department recently succeeded in the allocation of the 40MHz frequency for surface vehicle users – boats and cars – and there are thirty slots available. Sets in this band are now generally available at a higher price than 27MHz equipment due to the higher specification. However 27MHz is still by far and away the predominant band used by model boat enthusiasts and is likely to remain the major radio control frequency for many years.

As far as the UHF band is concerned, the comparative electronic sophistication required to make use of this band resulted in high prices. We say resulted as at the time of writing there is no company currently manufacturing equipment on this frequency, despite a number of attempts in the past.

Frequencies

We stated earlier the frequency band within which the 27MHz allocation is allowed is 26.960 to 27.280MHz. This band can be proportionally divided to allow for twelve sets of radio equipment to be operated simultaneously without interfering with each other. This extremely precise frequency control can be maintained by the most sophisticated circuitry, but this would be extremely expensive and has only become possible comparatively recently with the advent of microprocessor controlled circuits. So how has this precision been achieved ever since the introduction of super-heterodyne circuitry some twenty years ago? The secret lies in a naturally occurring mineral called quartz. This mineral can be ground using precision machinery to different shapes and different shapes will vibrate at only one specific frequency determined by the shape when subjected to an electric current.

In the early days of crystals, most sets of gear were sold with only one set of crystals (a set contains two crystals) – one is required for the transmitter and a corresponding matched crystal for the transmitter, and these were usually a permanent fixture in the equipment, being soldered in situ. It is normal practice today though for crystals to be interchangeable so it is simply a matter of plugging the correct matching pair into their respective sockets on the transmitter and the receiver. It is important to make certain that the transmitter crystal only goes into the transmitter and vice-versa. Incorrect fitting will drastically reduce the range of the equipment and move the frequency into an illegal operating band. In order to make it easy to identify the frequency in use for personal and other modellers' benefit – remember only one frequency can be operated at one and the same time, otherwise severe interference will result – it has been agreed in the United Kingdom that each 27MHz transmitter should carry a flag or pennant of certain colours. The six 'solid' colours, sometimes also known as 'spots' were the maximum number of frequencies that could be simultaneously operated when crystal controlled equipment first appeared, but most equipment sold today can successfully operate on closer frequency tolerances, although difficulties can still occur when operating with older gear that was not designed for such precise use. The later seven frequencies were fitted in between the 'solids' and came to be known as 'splits'. It is important to understand that the transmitter and receiver crystals are not the same frequency, but they differ by an amount which is equal to the intermediate frequency of the receiver. This is a frequency generated by the receiver to improve its selectivity. The value

An example of the latest in R/C equipment which features computer controlled pre-programming and modular systems. The former allows the equipment to be configured for different models: the latter allows one to change frequency ranges easily. This equipment, little used in the UK, is more common in Europe.

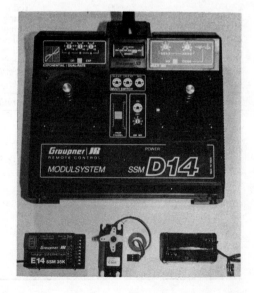

Receiver MHz	Transmitter MHz	Colour
British		
26.975	26.520	grey/brown
26.995	26.540	brown
27.025	26.570	brown/red
27.045	26.590	red
27.075	26.620	red/orange
27.095	26.640	orange
27.125	26.670	orange/yellow
27.145	26.690	yellow
27.175	26.720	yellow/green
27.195	26.740	green
27.225	26.770	green/blue
27.255	26.800	blue
German		
26.975	26.515	grey/brown
26.995	26.535	brown
27.025	26.565	brown/red
27.045	26.585	red
27.075	26.615	red/orange
27.095	26.635	orange
27.125	26.665	orange/yellow
27.145	26.685	yellow
27.175	26.715	yellow/green
27.195	26.735	green
27.255	26.765	green/blue
27.285	26.795	blue
American and Japanese		
26.970	26.500	grey/brown
26.995	26.525	brown
27.020	26.550	brown/red
27.045	26.575	red
27.070	26.600	red/orange
27.095	26.625	orange
27.120	26.650	orange/yellow
27.145	26.675	yellow
27.170	26.700	yellow/green
27.195	26.725	green
27.220	26.750	green/blue
27.245	26.775	blue

Transmitter MHz	Number	Transmitter MHz	Number
40.665	665	40.815	815
40.675	675	40.825	825
40.685	685	40.835	835
40.695	695	40.845	845
40.705	705	40.855	855
40.715	715	40.865	865
40.725	725	40.875	875
40.735	735	40.885	885
40.745	745	40.895	895
40.755	755	40.905	905
40.765	765	40.915	915
40.775	775	40.925	925
40.785	785	40.935	935
40.795	795	40.945	945
40.805	805	40.955	955

is usually 470KHz in America and 455KHz in Japan.

40MHz transmitters also carry a flag which is of one colour, green, but which has the frequency number shown to differentiate from other users. The recommendations are shown in the table.

When first purchased your crystals will be either in small plastic holders or be wrapped with a plastic sleeve to identify them. Should these identifiers become lost or damaged you will note that the metal crystal cases have their frequency stamped on them. The table will enable identification to take place as to which is transmitter and which is receiver for the desired frequency.

These separate lists highlight the fact that only crystals supplied by specific manufacturers of a particular make of equipment should be used and they should not be intermixed.

We warned earlier against model shops that advise that 35MHz can be used by boaters. From reading the above, some modellers may consider that surely it is just a simple case of using 35 or 40MHz band crystals in 27MHz band equipment and vice-versa. Unfortunately the large difference between the frequency bands means that different component values have to be used in the receiver and transmitter circuits and the equipment will not function at all if this modification is attempted. A number of manufacturers do now produce modular systems though, which allow a range of different frequency bands to be utilised. The transmitter and the receiver have holes in their cases where a module can be inserted which allows operation on the selected frequency band. These systems are still relatively expensive and can only really be justified if you intend to take up aircraft and boat modelling, or intend to use your equipment overseas where 27 or 40MHz may not be allowed.

Multi channel or functions

Multi-channel or multi-function systems were mentioned in chapter one and it is pertinent at this point to discuss requirements in more detail. The term 'channel' is seldom used today and is a hangover from the time of reed and tone equipment where one channel or tone operated the relay and then the servo or actuating mechanism in one direction only. The more accepted term used today is 'function' which means precisely what it says. A function describes the total movement of one control surface, i.e., one function will control the entire rudder movement and another function will look after the throttle on a power boat or the winch system of a yacht.

Obviously, therefore, most model boat requirements can be met by 'two-function' equipment. Such items as trim tabs or carburettor mixture controls on power boats or separate jib and mainsail control on yachts will require three functions. Four-function would look after rudder and throttle control plus other functions on a scale model such as fire hydrants, winches, bow thrusters, lights, cranes, etc. If the latter, that is fully operational scale models, is your interest, then you should search out some of the very specialist radio control equipment, mainly from West Germany, which specialises in microprocessor controlled systems which can operate large numbers of such accessories in pre-programmed sequences or individually. Of course the more sophisticated the control and the number of functions, the more expensive is the equipment. One can of course buy a four-function outfit with only two servos and add the others at a later stage. It is very necessary though to examine possible future requirements, and if a two-function outfit is adequate, then there is little point in spending extra for further functions. It would be more sensible to spend the extra finance on the best that can be afforded that will fill the bill.

Mode

The mode or manner in which the transmitter sticks are laid out on the transmitter face is worth considering. As radio systems were initially developed to control model aeroplanes, the normal arrangement for a two-function system would be to have both functions controlled by one stick which is pivoted in two axes, controlling both functions simultaneously. Most model boaters with two-function gear will prefer to have this one stick replaced by two single sticks which can only move

A cross-section through a typical modern servo showing the electronic and mechanical sophistication. It measures approximately 40mm in length.

horizontally or vertically. The normally accepted mode for model boat operation is to have the horizontal stick on the right of the transmitter controlling the rudder, with the left mounted vertical stick controlling the throttle on a power boat or the sheeting system on a yacht. For a three-function system, one stick would have the universal aircraft mode mentioned earlier; four function would have two such sticks.

Sticks can be self-centring, that is they always return to the neutral position when released – this is the normal set-up for a rudder – or they can be fitted with a ratchet friction system which maintains the stick in the position last set. This method would be used for the throttle or winch operation.

The trims, mentioned briefly earlier, usually consist of a small lever adjacent to each stick, which provide approximately 10% of the servo movement in the direction in which the trim lever is moved, independent of the main lever stick. This gives the facility of adjusting the servo neutral to give an exact straight line on a rudder or minutely adjust the throttle response during model operation. The trim should not be used to counteract bad servo installation practice.

Special servo units

The standard servos are suitable for most installations that beginners will require in scale boats and most power boats as far as the primary function is concerned, that of rudder. They will also suit practically all throttle applications on an internal combustion engined model. For scale models, the vast majority of which are electric motor powered, some form of speed controlling device will be needed. A standard servo can be used to operate a mechanical speed controller or even switch micro-switches, but sooner or later most modellers turn to a fully electronic type of controller which replaces the servo and plugs directly

The Whirlwind sail winch is small but has achieved a fine reputation and is widely used on R/C yachts in Britain and elsewhere.

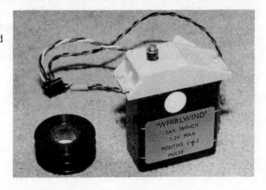

into the receiver. The major advantage of these electronic controllers is their ability to provide full proportional control over the entire speed range of the motor, usually both forward and astern. The output circuits have to handle quite large currents and the circuitry is relatively sophisticated. However, there are a number of simpler circuits which provide reasonable control for low power models and these will be discussed in more detail in the relevant chapter.

Model yachts will require a special kind of 'beefed up' servo which turns a drum which in turn winds a cord in or out and the cord is attached to the sails of the model, so letting them in or out according to the wind conditions. Quite often the drum will be split into two separate parts of different diameter. This arrangement can give different winding speeds and travels for the main and the jib. Although these units also plug directly into the receiver, they often require an additional separate battery supply as the electrical demand is relatively high, especially in strong winds. The unit resembles a small winch which is precisely what it is called.

What to buy

There are a number of questions to ask yourself before purchase:–
(a) Number of functions required?
(b) Dry cell or nicads?
(c) Number of servos or special units?
(d) Servicing facilities acceptable?
(e) Frequency band?
(f) Frequency tolerance, i.e., will it operate on 'splits'?
(g) Is it to a standard that will accept other manufacturer's peripherals – speed controllers and winches?

If you are completely new to radio control, some of the questions above will still be unanswerable at this stage, but hopefully by the time you come to the end of this book you will be armed with enough knowledge to be in a position to discuss the technicalities of your purchase on equal terms with the model shop proprietor and end up with exactly the right equipment for your present and future needs. The right start to any hobby usually means sailing off into the future with confidence, rather than giving it all up as a frustratingly bad job.

The model

3

The choice of subject for a radio controlled model is much more difficult than the choosing of the radio control equipment. But there is one over-riding piece of advice at this stage, and that is don't wait. Make the decision and do something about it. Hopefully this chapter will ease the decision-making process.

Helping to choose

There is nothing to beat obtaining advice from a reliable source and if you are fortunate enough to have a good model shop proprietor who values his long-term customers then that is certainly a good place to start at. You might be even more fortunate and have a club in your locality. For most modellers this is indeed a godsend and will almost invariably influence your decision as to the type of model to build. After all, there is not much point in making a power boat if the club's prime interest is scale or yachts and vice-versa. If you have a burning desire for a particular type of model you can always join the club and follow the majority interest until the time comes when you can bring some pressure to bear to include your own desire. But don't expect to walk into the local club and change their ways overnight. There may well be very important reasons as to why the club operates the models that it does: possibly the owner of the water is not keen on internal combustion engine powered models or there is a noise embargo. Join in and find out. If you are not aware of a local group try asking at the public library, or you could write to one of the modelling magazines, including an s.a.e., for the name and address of the secretary of your nearest group. It must be said that you will learn more from an enthusiastic bunch of fellow modellers in less than half the time it takes to read this book! Do beware of the local club knowall, though – he could get you into bad ways.

Many newcomers will have some idea in their mind as to what they want to model. This may have been inspired by having seen a similar

Scale models come in all shapes and sizes. This magnificent model of HMS *Vanguard* took its builder 15000 hours, and is scratchbuilt from shipyard drawings. She has been featured on television and has won major awards throughout the country. (Photo courtesy Ulster Television).

model at a show or regatta, or the wish to produce a model for family or personal reasons – perhaps a close relation has served on a particular vessel – or one may have seen a prototype in a film or on TV. There are now enough model boaters in this country for all members of the population to have seen a model boat in operation, and even the media have at long last realised that models can be very useful in films and television work. It is much more economical to blow up a model ship than a real one and the art of the model-maker is now very much appreciated by producers and directors. The science-fiction film industry would also cease to exist without skilled and talented model-makers.

The choice between power, wind or scale can also be affected by the local water availability, even if a club has not obtained the right to use it. If you live in a town where the only water is shallow, say less than 500mm deep, and surrounded by trees and/or buildings, then it is going to be pretty useless for sailing a yacht. Also, due to the proximity of houses then again the environmental problem arises. Internal com-

Above, big and small – the choice is yours. This superb little modern harbour tug *is* radio controlled and sails very well.

Right, young and old can enjoy model boating. This junior scale enthusiast regularly sails his Pilot Boat in competitions.

Below, tugs are the most popular scale subject. This is *Hibernia* performing at a recent World Championship.

Above, lifeboats are not uncommon subjects since plans are available from commercial sources as well as the RNLI.

Left, period steam launches have been rapidly gaining popularity over recent years, as has steam propulsion for models generally.

Below, merchant ships have tended to be ignored by modellers, but more are now being seen. Plans can be a problem.

Fishing boats are very popular subjects, giving great scope for detail and atmospheric work and proving seaworthy at almost any size.

bustion engined models will just not be acceptable. The only resort will be scale or perhaps competition electrics.

However, even what initially seems a great stretch of water for sailing a model boat is probably restricted to other users or is again environmentally protected because of bird life or even fishing groups. A bad fisherman will do more harm to the fish and bird life than a bad

Paddlers have a fascinating attraction as the paddle wheels throb with life. This scratch-built *Medway Queen* relives the Sunday afternoon pleasure trip.

By diligent research some very unusual subjects can be found, such as this Whitby Dredger. Plans for this model are now available commercially among the hundreds in Model Boats Plans Service.

model boater but that's another issue. You are more likely to find a model yachting group operating in such a location.

If you really do want to join the internal combustion engined fraternity it is more than likely that you will be forced to find your nearest group and perhaps be prepared to travel some distance to be able to pursue your hobby.

If this all sounds rather disheartening it is better to be aware of such potential difficulties before you build a jet powered *Bluebird*. By building an acceptable model for the prevailing conditions you will avoid aggravation and frustration.

Choosing

At first sight it seems quite bewildering to a newcomer as to the wide variety of types of model boat activities he/she has available to choose. It is very easy to be pushed into building something that wasn't quite what you had in mind by an over-enthusiastic modeller or model shop proprietor. The best advice here is to say don't just take one person's advice – shop around – think about the ramifications and requirements.

The large bewildering choice can be broken down into a number of categories and sub-categories which will make your decisions much easier.

Submarines bring many difficulties, not the least of which is keeping the water out. This scratch-built model is performing in front of a very interested crowd at a regatta held in a swimming pool.

The most important piece of advice is start simple, and by simple we mean something that is within your capabilities. Unfortunately one of the hardest tasks for most human beings is in analysing their own abilities. Most of us tend to think we are more able than we actually are, particularly with practical skills. Like everything else in life, you cannot run before you can walk. We hate to think how many fine modellers have been lost over the years by the newcomer trying to model a

Stand-off scale models can look superb on the water, despite the compromise in detail. This WWII CAMship is also available from Model Boats Plans Service.

Victory or *Hood* as their first model and soon becoming frustrated and disillusioned. You will still need to develop most of the skills required to build a *Victory* for a less ambitious model, but by starting off with something less demanding, the fruits of your labours quickly become apparent and one is motivated towards completion and satisfaction. Then is the time to consider the big one!

Before moving on to discuss the various categories it can be stated that there are very few ship or boat models that will not accept the standard radio control equipment available today. The lower size limit is probably around 8 to 10in in length. It is possible to radio control much smaller models, but the newcomer should go for a model not less than 15 to 18in. There is no real upper limit, except for weights and lengths that can be manhandled and are safe to operate.

Classifications

At this stage we can break the various types into classifications and discuss them in more detail. Practically all models can be split into the two major categories of Power and Sail.

Power can be sub-divided into scale models, powered by electric or internal combustion engines, and 'power models' in their own right. The latter term has come to mean models that are designed solely to function in a manner that makes them ideal for the task in hand – for example racing or performing intricate steering manoeuvres against the clock.

Scale models

The variety of choice is overwhelming – from tugs to trawlers, warships to merchant ships, boats to barges, lifeboats to submarines, inshore harbour craft to oil tankers, diving support ships to coasters, etc., etc. You are certainly spoilt for choice.

At the decision stage it is important to consider the subject of personal transport. We do know of one or two eccentric modellers who have built ingenious transportation trailers to tow behind their bicycles, but most will be using some form of motor car or public transport. It must be said from the outset that public transport is far from ideal and you will not be popular unless the model is well protected in its own box or travelling container. This obviously limits its size somewhat. Before the days of personal transport many clubs had purpose-made store houses at their waters and the models seldom travelled anywhere except from boat-house to water and hopefully back again at the end of the session.

Recently tug towing competitions have become popular where a team of two modellers have to manoeuvre a large tow such as a tanker around a course resembling an estuary or harbour. Below, scale regattas in GB usually involve steering a model around a course which resembles an estuary or harbour. Here a coaster passes a stationary lightship. (Photos Ray Brigden).

Demonstration events to large public audiences are very popular in Europe, and are slowly gathering a following in Great Britain. This 18ft long container ship built by a Dutch model group has just received its pilot prior to being towed into harbour. Below, an indoor view of the bows of the ship, showing her bow thruster, and two tugs, the latter about 30in long.

There are still a few clubs with this facility, but the problem they suffer with today is one of vandalism.

Even with own personal transport don't build an 8ft long destroyer if you only have a Mini. It has been known. Also, a rigged model yacht or sailing ship can be the devil of a job to squeeze into the back of even quite a large car. Think logistics before committing yourself.

As to motive power the large majority of ship and boat modellers use electric propulsion. This has many advantages over other forms of propulsion, particularly for scale models. It is clean, very controllable and relatively inexpensive to operate and maintain. The widespread use of nickel-cadmium rechargeable cells has revolutionised the use of electric power for models over recent years. They are relatively maintenance and trouble free and last for many years. They have also had a marked effect on high performance racing models. We will take a closer look at these power sources later.

You may be quite happy to make use of your radio control equipment to allow you to operate your scale model realistically and bring it back to the operating point on completion of the outing, rather than chase it around the lake rescuing it from reeds, etc., with a fishing rod. This form of radio controlled operation is very relaxing and constitutes by far the largest use of equipment.

Many, however, soon tire of motoring aimlessly around the lake and start to steer around natural hazards or even lay out one or two artificial hazards to steer around. Some also enjoy the competitive spirit. All this can be brought together with scale models at local club level, and if the

Modern internal combustion engined multi-boats are fast, around 35 to 40mph, streamlined and stable. All use grp hulls.

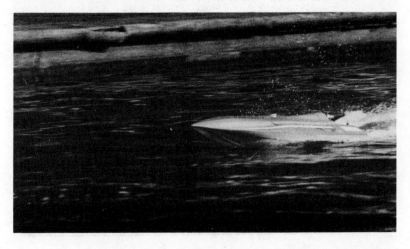

need arises the keener competitor can move on to national, international and even world competition.

Most club competitions follow the format where models are steered around a navigational course, usually representing full-size hazards such as marker buoys, lighthouses, wrecks, etc. Points are lost for striking hazards or negotiating the course in the wrong direction, and points are gained for correct traversing of the course. The styles of courses vary quite widely in the United Kingdom and no two regattas are exactly alike. This is contrary to most events held on the Continent which use a standard triangular shaped course. The latter does have the advantage that all competitors start off on an equal footing, but it can be very boring for spectators and ultimately for competitors. But it must also be said that if we are to do well as a competing nation in international competitions then some of the events in this country need to be organised on international lines in order for our competitors to gain experience of the particular European courses. The navigational hazard type course is certainly more attractive and interesting and recently some European countries have begun to use similar arrangements. There is obviously room for a coming together to obtain the best of both worlds.

Most events do not restrict the size of the model – either minimum or maximum – and many modellers have recently been searching for prototypes which are better suited to regatta operation. Initially one may consider that a small model would have considerable advantage in being more manoeuvrable and easier to pass between the buoys. This is certainly the case on pleasant, calm days, but things are a little different in rough weather; and unfortunately conditions are more likely to be the latter in the United Kingdom.

Offshore multi-boats are not quite as fast but are nevertheless very spectacular and exciting to drive in sea conditions. They also need to be well protected from salty sea water.

The recent trend has been towards larger models of modern ships which are fitted with propulsion systems such as steerable rudders or bow thrusters which make them very manoeuvrable. Suitable subjects are oil rig support ships and modern tugs. Because of the increasing manoeuvrability of these models, regatta course designers have been inexorably moving towards tighter and tighter courses, to the detriment of the larger model, of course. The continental system goes a little way towards resolving this problem by splitting the entries into classes depending upon their length, but this is hardly feasible for local regattas. The governing body, the Model Power Boat Association, is currently studying suggestions for reversing this trend towards smaller, specialised models. Fortunately, though, there is an enormous, indeed almost endless, supply of prototypes which guarantees a cross-section of very different models at most events.

When considering choice of a prototype, therefore, one can also choose any type ship, but if competition is to be enjoyed then don't go too small (below 12in) and try for a design that will steer reasonably well when going astern. The reason for the latter is that most events employ an astern maneouvre, a much more difficult operation than it first appears. All ships will move astern; it becomes a different state of affairs though when trying to steer between a pair of buoys. No hard and fast examples can be given as all models seem to behave differently. Even two identical models can behave as though they come from different moulds.

If you intend to become a serious competitor in scale steering competitions there is one important thing that will give great help to successful navigation whatever the model or courses; that is to know your model's quirks completely. Throw a couple of buoys out about 1 metre apart every time you get the opportunity and practise going through them forward and particularly astern and prescribing various circles of large and small radii around them. Also practise berthing alongside, as many competitions require a docking sequence. When docking you will need to allow for the swing of the ship induced by the torque effect of the screw. With an anti-clockwise turning propeller, when viewed from astern, it is best to approach the dock from the left, that is starboard side to the quay, and vice-versa for a clockwise turning propeller. Many modellers consider that two screws will be of advantage in steering competitions. Unless the two propellers can be individually and precisely controlled for revolutions, there will be no advantage over a single screw.

It is obvious from much of the foregoing that precise control of the propeller speed is required for successful competition use. This is very true and for anything more than fun club competition an electronic speed controller is essential. For twin screw ships it is possible to run

A world class 3.5cc grp multi-boat from Italian master of the art, Giorgio Merlotti. Engine mounted on noise reducing dampers, large tank, tuned exhaust pipe and completely sealed radio compartment at rear.

both screws from one speed controller, but it is hardly likely that both motors will be electrically identical and operate at exactly the same speed, particularly at low revolutions, which is precisely where accurate revolution control is required. Also, many modern ships incorporate a bow thruster and while it is not usual to fit sophisticated speed control on this unit, at least another function is required on your radio control equipment. So remember to take the above considerations into account before purchasing your equipment.

A final consideration for modellers intending to compete in top level competition is to be aware that their models must not only be capable of being steered successfully around the navigational course; they will be judged for scale fidelity, accuracy and quality of construction, finish, etc. Models for international competition must also be no longer than 250cm and no shorter than 70cm. Further details concerning the rules and categories can be obtained from the Model Power Boat Association. See chapter 12.

A large percentage of modellers do not or cannot build models to these standards, so this major group are accommodated within the semi-scale or stand-off categories. This would be a model of a scale prototype but which does not include every last detail and which looks correct at 7 to 10 yards distance. Hence it is judged at such a distance, therefore stand-off.

At international level, with boats equipped to perform more than just steering, i.e. those with special operating functions, there is a special class where a competitor has 10 minutes to perform a freelance but programmed sequence of manoeuvres, and earn points for execution of the programme from a jury. There is also a category where a number of modellers can join forces to put on a display which will be similarly adjudged. Such events can be very spectacular and include sinking ships and their recovery, fires on oil rigs extinguished by support ships, sea battles, etc. Large audiences from the general public as well as modellers are attracted to such displays.

Power models

The categorisation can be split into 'sport' and 'racing' models. The former are usually launch or cabin-cruiser type models of hard chine or planing hull design. They can be powered by electric or internal combustion engines and are used primarily for fun running rather than competition. There are a wide variety of designs available in both plan and kit forms.

Racing models

The vast majority of the classifications raced in the UK are based on those operated by the World Model Boating Federation NAVIGA. This organisation was formed in the 1950s as a European body and became a World Federation in 1980, the only major exceptions being North America and Canada, although it is hoped they will ultimately also join.

NAVIGA racing classifications are now followed almost world-wide, although most participating countries tend to add domestic categories of their own as and when the need arises. The Americans run a form of racing using radio controlled hydroplanes which are extremely fast and good spectator material. There are now a number of clubs and individuals in this country and on the Continent starting to operate these models and NAVIGA hosted a championship for these models in 1986. At least three weekends of hydro racing are now organised in the United Kingdom.

The classifications discussed here will be confined to the NAVIGA groupings covering radio control. All NAVIGA R/C classes are prefixed with the letter F.

Speed events are F1 and are run around a 30 metre triangular course, one lap in each direction. This course involves 60 degree turns and one of 180 degrees, requiring a boat capable of fast turns and acceleration as well as fast straight line speed; the fastest times on this course are around 12 seconds.

F1 is divided into F1V (internal combustion) and F1E (electric) categories as follows:

F1V-3.5	up to 3.5cc engines
F1V-6.5	3.51 to 6.5cc engines
F1V-15	6.51 to 15cc engines
F1E-1kg	electric boats weighing up to 1kg
F1E-+1kg	electric boats limited only to 42 volts

Steering events are F3 and are divided into F3V and F3E for internal combustion and electric powered boats respectively. This form of steering is for functional models, not scale models. The course is again based on the 30 metre triangle, (see appendix 1) and the boats must follow the prescribed course cleanly without touching the buoys and as fast as possible. The boats tend to be small, fast, and very agile. There is no restriction on size, but since the marker buoys are only placed 1 metre apart, small boats have a natural advantage. A typical F3V boat would measure 20-22in long, with a 3.5cc engine, and would complete a clear round in under 35 seconds.

A typical F3E boat would be about the same size, using nickel-cadmium fast rechargeable batteries and weighing just over 1kg, and would only be a second or so slower over the same course.

Certainly the most popular power racing categories are those concerned with multi-racing, the FSR classes. These boats travel at remarkably fast speeds around a 220 metre M shaped course, and when

Three-point R/C hydroplanes are very fast – average 60mph, can do 90+ – and originated in America, although classifications now exist in NAVIGA and GB and interest is growing. Normally wood construction with foam filled sponsons.

Another racing boat popular in America now trickling into GB is the scale hydroplane – usually sporting an immaculate paint job.

12 models are battling it out things can get very fast and furious. The race lengths vary from 30 minutes up to 1 hour and 2 hour endurance racing. Exceptionally well maintained, reliable and fast but tough boats are required to survive, and the drivers need to be aggressive when necessary but patient and skilful to take full advantage of the changing conditions of a race.

Most, if not all, racers make use of commercially available glass reinforced plastic hulls, commonly but incorrectly referred to as fibreglass. These are available from a number of manufacturers and there is a whole world of specialist fittings to equip the boats. A number of suppliers sponsor works teams as in full-size power boat racing. The categories are:–

FSR-3.5	engines up to 3.5cc
FSR-6.5	engines between 3.51 and 6.54cc
FSR-15	engines between 6.55 and 15cc
FSR-35	petrol fuelled engines between 15 and 35cc

The advent of fast rechargeable nickel-cadmium cells has led to the development of electric multi-racing, and the UK was a major instigator of these events. Races are for 15 minutes and 10 minutes respectively in:

FSRE-2kg	boat and cells to be under 3kg
FSRE-Un1	no restriction except 42 volts maximum

At present the NAVIGA organisation holds a World Championship every two years for power events, but split into multi and speed/steering

Start of an electric multi-race for boats weighing up to 2 kilos; running time 10 minutes. Electric racing is only slightly slower than the equivalent i.c. class but is usually close and full of spills as the boats are more evenly matched.

events. The championships normally alternate between East and West European countries. Despite being a world organisation, so far only one event has been held outside Europe, in China in 1989.

An exciting moment from a 12 boat electric multi-race at a recent World Championships – 7 boats in shot.

Fast electric boats designed for speed events are built extremely light with carbon fibre/epoxy shells and thin acetate film for hatch covers.

There are many other types of event held throughout the entire country every weekend from March till October, and variety is the name of the game. There are classes specifically to help the beginner, and many clubs run inter-league matches with others in their immediate area. Some events are restricted to commercial products up to a certain price limit to keep operating costs at a minimum.

Yachts

The aesthetic appeal of a model yacht is very strong and many novices consider the yacht to be an easy subject. This is far from the truth and the design of a model yacht is as complex an undertaking as the design of a full-size yacht. The newcomer is very strongly advised to start off with an approved design, whether it be one of the many plans published or from a kit. The term 'kit' as accepted in most of the modelling world has only recently reached this stage in model yachting. It is still not easy, however, to find a model shop stocking the complete range of model yacht kits, hulls and fittings and it will probably be necessary for the potential model yachtsman to do a bit more shopping around than the power boat modeller.

Scale sailing craft

Many newcomers will wish to build a scale sailing model and it must be said at this point that one would be embarking on the most difficult subject in the world of model boating. The reason is a question of scale. Consider a model built to a scale of 1:8 of the prototype. Its length will certainly be 1:8, however the sail area will be 1:64 whilst the all important displacement or volume will only be a 512th of the original. It is not difficult to see that the model would be sailing in the full-size

47

medium at a considerable disadvantage. The larger the model, hence the smaller the scale factor, the better. Some fore and aft rigged models are satisfactory but square riggers will only travel off the wind and are extremely complicated to rig from radio control equipment. One answer is to cheat with the displacement factor by fitting a larger than scale volume below the keel to give extra side area and allow for a larger ballast. Such a false keel can be made easily removable so as not to detract from the model's static display state.

Functional and racing yachts

The question of size has a bearing on functional fore and aft rigged yachts. A 36in long yacht will seem gigantic in the workshop or in the car but when on the water it will soon be realised that with one or two exceptions, it is the smallest feasible size for adequate performance in all-round conditions.

The lightest radio gear today will weigh around 1lb and in a large model displacing some 40lbs it is going to be insignificant. However with a yacht weighing 5lb, the radio weight is 20% of the whole and consequently the all-important ballast of the boat is markedly reduced.

The benefits of 40MHz; 19 yachts attempt a race in very light wind conditions. (Photo: Mike Kemp).

Multi-hull boats are fast but suffer badly from gusts and tripping – that is digging in of the bows and subsequent capsizing. Right, an IMYRU specification One Metre yacht, the *Impala,* distributed by Kip Marketing. (Photo: Chris Jackson).

5lbs is going to be the lowest weight that a model could possibly be constructed at to carry radio equipment, and the laws of physics will allow this weight to displace nearly 140cu. in of water. The laws of hyrodynamics also result in faster speeds for less power required for longer hull lengths, or to be more correct, longer waterline lengths. Our 5lb boat could just about be stretched to 30in, which is therefore a reasonable minimum recommended length for a model yacht.

The main advantage for wishing to remain small, apart from the transportation problem mentioned earlier (but that can be overcome) is that a conventional servo can be used to control the sails instead of the much more expensive sail winch. However, the only class that has obtained even a moderate degree of success at a small size is the 22in long Duplex 575, but even this, at its smaller than recommended length, sometimes cannot be turned through the wind in strong gusts because the standard servo does not have enough torque to pull the sails in against the wind strength. The model cannot be sailed in very strong winds either, even with its smaller suit of sails fitted. Despite these deficiences, though, the class has introduced many people to the fun of radio controlled model yachts and continues to have a strong following. If you already possess a two-function outfit then the 575 is a good way of experiencing the world of model yachting without too much expenditure. But if you have not yet purchased your R/C gear and model yachting is your wish then buy a winch at the outset instead of a second servo.

Early days

Model yachts were more than likely the first ever working models and clubs were in existence in this country and America over 100 years ago. Competitions usually took the form of two competitors racing one another from one end of the lake to the other in a series of boards. Self steering mechanisms which slightly changed the direction of the rudder as the wind changed became extremely sophisticated and were in fact studied very closely by the round the world single handed yachtsmen such as Sir Francis Chichester.

Model yachting probably called out more for radio than any other branch of our hobby, but the strong yet fast acting winch mechanism to operate the sails was a long time coming. Also it must be said that the controlling bodies were a little conservative with regards to radio control – the MPBA was no exception on the power boat side – and it was as late as 1972 before the yachting associations accepted radio classes. There was immediate expansion and radio models now far outstrip non-radio models throughout the world.

Classes

As with the power boat classifications there is a world governing association called IMYRU, the International Model Yacht Racing Union, founded in 1927, and its classes and rules are used by all nations. Again, as per the power boaters, many countries have local classes to suit special conditions. The body for England and Wales is the Model Yachting Association – Scotland has its own body – and the following is a synopsis of the classes followed in the United Kingdom.

RM Radio Marblehead – limited to an overall length of 50in plus or minus .25in and with a total sail area of 800sq. in. The yachts average 12-18lb in total weight and there are few other restrictions. The Marblehead is the most popular class in this country and throughout the world.

R10r Radio 10 rater – this class produces the fastest and usually longest models, often up to 7ft long and very slim. The governing rule concerns waterline length and sail area in the ratio of:

$$\frac{SA \times LWL}{7500} = 10$$

The dimensions are in inches and it is obvious that a longer boat can be obtained at the expense of less sail area and vice-versa. A 55in boat would have a sail area of 1363sq. in and a 72in boat some 1041sq. in. Typical displacement would be around 20 to 24lb.

RA – the largest and one of the oldest classes with a complicated formula which nevertheless results in a wide variety of designs with equable performances. Displacement can vary from 20 to 90lb, but an average yacht would be 50lb on a 55in waterline with 1500sq. in of sail. The class has not transferred to radio as successfully as the RM and R10rs, but still has a strong following in this country particularly.

R36R Radio Restricted – a British class although there is a close equivalent in the United States called the 36/600. The simple requirement of this class is that the hull must fit into a box measuring 36 × 11 × 9in and total weight must not exceed 12lb. Sail area is unlimited. This class is now very popular and a number of kits have appeared recently. It makes a good transition from the smaller 575 class or as a first model.

One Metre – a relatively new class that offers convenient size and fast, exciting, racing. Likely to become as popular as the RM category.

EC 12m – stands for East Coast 12 Metre with the rules recently tidied up by IMYRU. This one-design class creates boats around 60in long and displacement of 26.5lbs. The class is very popular in the USA, but there is little interest in the UK.

6 Metre – another class under IMYRU rules. Formula is similar to that used for full-sized Americas Cup races; results in boats between 55 to 65in long and 25lbs displacement. It has a small UK following.

575 – the smallest class and only really suited to moderate winds, but nevertheless one that has introduced hundreds to radio yachting. Major advantage is that a servo will handle the sails and transportation is easy. A slightly larger successor, the 590 is now available from the original designer.

Radio controlled yachts are usually raced in 6 to 12 boat heats over a triangular course or sometimes the Olympic course, see appendix 1. Two laps are usually covered and the models given points for finishing. Sometimes the entries are split up into fleets and after each heat the top two competitors move up a fleet and the bottom two move down.

Still the most popular class worldwide, the 50in Marbleheads are fast, exciting to race and reasonably easy to transport. There are a number of kits, hulls and plans available.

The main object of the rules for each class is to create a group of models that are close enough in their performance to give close racing, yet leave designers enough freedom to improve classes without resulting in overwhelming development. All this basically means that it is the best skipper who wins and that there is a strong emphasis on sailing ability rather than depth of pocket to purchase the latest design.

Whether your interest is scale, power boat racing or sailing, the maximum enjoyment will be obtained in competing with fellow enthusiasts of like mind, and it is the objective of all the rules and regulations to provide a fair environment for all to enjoy their chosen hobby at whatever level of expertise and to foster relaxation and enjoyment of model boating in all its competitive aspects.

The unusual

Not all modellers wish to conform and without the experimenter or the person who desires to model something completely different it would be a dull world.

Submarines are a particular example. They are attractive propositions and many newcomers are keen to start their modelling career with one.

The advice is don't – until you have a successful working conventional model under your belt. Submarines operate in three dimensions and need four primary controls; rudder, motor speed, hydrovane for diving trim and some system of altering the ballast for diving and surfacing.

Radio control is maintained for depths of up to 2 metres at a distance of some 10 metres, provided the aerial wire is completely insulated from the surrounding water. Complete watertightness of the radio and drive gear is essential and not easy to achieve, and finally some failsafe system is necessary to bring the submarine to the surface on loss of control.

There is a national association of model submariners whose address can be obtained from the MPBA, see appendix.

Airscrew boats

These are usually light high speed planing craft driven by an air cooled model aircraft engine. They are not really man enough to carry radio unless built large with correspondingly larger engines. The problem is

Scale sailing models are among the most difficult subjects because of the cube law. Prototypes need a relatively large and stable displacement to work well. The Thames Barge is one of the few suitable.

The kit-built 17in long 575 is the smallest racing class. It uses a servo instead of a sail winch and can perform surprisingly well in light to moderate winds. It has been responsible for introducing many model yachtsmen to the hobby.

one of safety, especially on lakes open to public access, and hence they are not accepted by the MPBA and many clubs.

Catamarans

The problem with the catamaran is that without the ability to change the weight distribution, as can be achieved with the full-size, it can easily capsize in a gust. This can also be caused by the tip of a float dipping and in effect somersaulting the boat. Devices such as spring-loaded masts which absorb the initial impact of the gust have been tried with some degrees of success. Model size is important again and the larger model is likely to be happier.

Finding out

We have already mentioned that you may be able to find out the whereabouts of your local club from your library or by writing to the model magazines. We have also listed the secretaries of the British associations in the appendix.

If you can't find a club, or even if you can, you should still read everything you can find on the subject. In addition to monthly magazines there are many books on modelling which should also be available from your library.

Some of these will be beyond the newcomer but as experience progresses, a lot of what is read will be of value and prove useful at a later stage.

Kit or scratch

4

It is an undisputed fact that the vast majority of modellers start off their modelling career with a kit. The choice today is very large as a visit to any model shop that at all specializes in marine modelling will soon confirm. It is also probably true to say that the British modeller has the largest and most varied choice than anywhere else in the world. We have the mass-produced German scale kits, French, Italian and Spanish products, Japanese plastics, some American and of course home-grown products from a variety of small and large manufacturers. British manufacturers now lead the world in quality and choice, and are particularly strong with respect to warships, merchant ships and working boats.

The United Kingdom is also a world leader in the manufacturer of glass reinforced plastic hulls, not only for scale models, but particularly of power boats and yachts. There are also still a number of manufacturers producing traditional kits based on all timber construction, some of which, as we mentioned in chapter one, were originally designed back in the early 1950s and which have more than stood the test of time.

Early days

At one time a kit was no more than a box of wood with the various sections for bulkheads, decks, etc., marked out and requiring cutting, sanding, etc. Even the most traditional kits today offer all the major components cut out – and many are die-cut, a precise method which guarantees accuracy and sharp edges – and the more prefabricated examples featured moulded hulls in styrene or ABS or glass reinforced plastic. Despite this intensive move to providing more and more of the kit in a nearly finished form, or perhaps because of it, as already mentioned, a number of manufacturers still provide the traditional style which requires the modeller to construct from the keel upwards in the time-honoured way.

Billing are probably the largest marine kit suppliers in the world and this is just a very small part of their vast range. Many are suitable for radio control and feature styrene hulls.

Choice

It would not be true to say that there is a kit to satisfy the exact requirements of all prospective builders, but there will be few who cannot find something of interest on the model shop shelves. A multitude of tugs and trawlers abound, plus offshore vessels, cabin cruisers, puffers, paddlers, police launches, yachts, fireboats, lifeboats, submarines and more recently, warships. Away from the scale side, at

Deans Marine is a relatively new British company which specialises in warship kits featuring grp hulls and grp/etched brass fittings. HMS *Skirmisher* is a typical example of their expanding range of kits.

The Robbe Scarab 38 is typical of the European approach to fast electric sports models. This features twin outdrives driven through the manufacturer's own gearboxes. Extensive pre-fabrication is utilised in these kits and every component is available from the manufacturer.

the functional end of things, there are grp hulls for all classes of power boats, both internal combustion and electric powered, and for most racing yacht classes. There are also a number of one-design yacht kits which have sold in large enough numbers to enable competitions to be organised.

For newcomers the same decisions with regards to choice of prototype need to be made much in keeping with the arguments given in the previous chapter. Scale or power, internal combustion or electric, or sail. Even having made that decision it is not just simply a case of rushing off to your nearest model shop and buying the first thing that appeals or which roughly conforms with what you had in mind. There are other criteria which still remain to be examined.

This is a British kit which comes complete with motor and batteries, from the H.F.M. Marine boatyard. Radio is not available from the manufacturer, but any modern outfit will be quite suitable. (Photo: Ray Brigden).

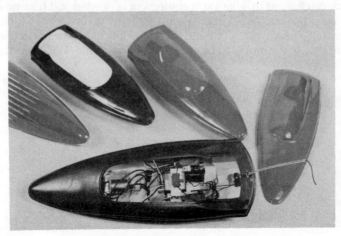

An epoxy/carbon fibre moulding for the restricted fast electric class. A number of manufacturers produce hulls for building up to the modeller's own wishes. This one is from Marine Dynamics.

Horses for courses

. . . or matching the chosen model to suit not only your desire but also, and more important, your ability and resources.

For a first model one should choose something fairly simple, and remember small is not necessarily simple, quite often the reverse. Also, if you are keen to get on the water quickly, then a model with a ready built hull would probably be a good idea. You should try and assess from a close inspection of the kit and particularly the instructions whether or not you have the time and enthusiasm to take the project to its conclusion.

The next thing is to make certain that any radio equipment or sources of power that you may already have in your possession and which you intend to use in your chosen model can in fact be made to suit. If you are starting from scratch then the opposite applies and you should check carefully as to what extra equipment is needed and how much it will cost. No kits include radio gear and only a very few include the drive motor. Also, many of the Continental kits require extra accessory kits to enable the model to be successfully completed. Usually today the

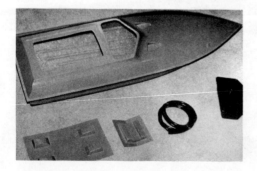

I.c. powered boats are also available as grp hulls, some with cockpit and exhaust vents to add a modicum of realism, particularly the off-shore category.

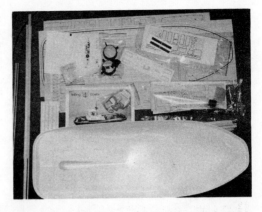

Most of the contents of the Billing *Smit Nederland* Dutch Tug kit. Features abs/styrene hull, ply decks and other miscellaneous parts.

running hardware (propeller shaft, rudder, etc.,) is included but not always. If it is included check that it is to a standard dimension so that spare propellers and shafts can be purchased later, or that the shop holds spare parts if they are non-standard. Propellers are readily available in a screw-on type in both 2 and 4mm sizes. Anything else is often difficult to locate spares for. What is practically never included is the so-called 'Fittings Kit', which includes all the hard to find detail fittings especially suited to the model in question, e.g. lights, bollards, cleats, winches, steering wheel, fire monitors, etc.

One way of trying to decide whether to go for all-timber built-up hull construction or towards the more prefabricated kit is to try and decide in your own mind if you are a carpenter or an engineer. The connection is obvious. Also, when reading the instruction booklet, look for

Many Continental kits require the purchase of an additional fittings/hardware kit. This is that required for the Billing *Smit Nederland*.

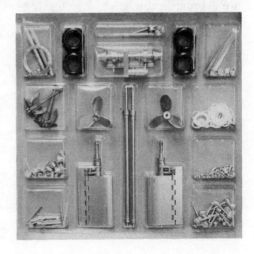

59

Calder Craft is an expanding British manufacturer with a range of attractive, typically British ships and boats featuring grp hulls and extremely high quality white metal fittings. This is the *North Light* Clyde Puffer.

references to skills that you do not at the time possess. Are the instructions good enough to teach you those skills? If not you are most certainly going to have considerable difficulty in constructing the model. Are special workshop tools required? Pretty important if you are working on the kitchen table!

The finished size of the model must also be considered at the purchase stage. It is often surprising how large a model can grow from a

And here is the finished kit packed with authenticity and detail, including crew on the wheelhouse bridge.

relatively small box, especially where a built-up hull is involved rather than a moulded hull, when size is pretty obvious. Have you somewhere convenient to store your model and is your means of transport capable of moving it from home to water?

Making a start

The big moment arrives! You have exploded the kit all over the work area and can't wait to get started. Hold on. Just sit back with the instructions and read them through, trying to identify as many components as possible, and then read them through again. If you don't do this, you will almost certainly rue those few minutes many times over during the next few days or weeks. This also gives you the opportunity to check if there are any parts missing, especially if a parts list is included which is more and more the case with recent kits.

The next stage is to try a dry run – that is assembling some of the major parts before gluing them together. Never apply any adhesive until you are absolutely certain that items are fitting together correctly. Don't rush and if not sure about something, reread the instructions.

The completed *Smit Nederland* from Billing is a very impressive model and is extremely manoeuvrable with the special Becker rudders and Kort nozzles.

For newcomers the plans and instructions are going to be a very important part of the kit. Most manufacturers are very aware that it will probably be the quality of their instructions that will tip many modellers's decisions for or against their kit, and because of that the quality is markedly better today than some years ago. However, don't assume that all kits meet such criteria. Ask to see the plans and instructions and choose an area of the construction that is not clear to you. Are the instructions clear, lucid, complete and accurate? If not – look for something else, however attractive the model is.

Competition kits

If yours is to be a competitive foray into model boating your choice will be obviously restricted as far as power and yacht categories are concerned. There is much less restriction appertaining to scale model choice. Practically every scale model on the commercial market will be acceptable at the vast majority of the regattas throughout the country, especially the growing number of clubs that separate kit models from scratchbuilt craft. The National Scale Championships have a kit category which is very well supported. For many years there was an unhealthy snobbish attitude by some scratchbuilders towards kit modellers. That has now almost disappeared and many of today's top scratchbuilders

Imara is probably the most detailed and most sophisticated kit currently available, a very impressive tug from the Calder Craft company. The boat features literally hundreds of superb white metal fittings on a glass fibre hull. (Photo: Ray Brigden).

Above, *Celia* is another kit from the Calder Craft range, this time featuring an abs/styrene hull. She is typical of a modern coastal and estuary fishing boat. Below, *Thyssen II* shows the ultra-sophistication creeping into German pre-fabricated kits. This Graupner offering features abs/styrene hull and propulsion is by two Schottel turbine blade units; their covers can be seen at the rear. The units are shown elsewhere.

These two HDMLs are scratchbuilt on abs/styrene hulls. Some modellers have difficlty in hull building and this approach avoids any problem. The hulls and plans are available from the Model Boats Plans Service.

will admit to having started their modelling career with a kit. Furthermore many now build kits during a long term scratch project to keep their enthusiasm alive. Some scratchbuilt boats will take many years to complete at national and international level.

The power boater will have the choice of a limited number of kits, or to be more accurate glass reinforced plastic hulls and ancillary components, for that is the way most internal combustion and some fast electrical model designs are marketed. The UK has an enviable reputation for the manufacture of top quality grp hulls, but the newcomer finds things a trifle difficult as until fairly recently the rest of the information towards assembling a racing boat has been less than easy to discover. A number of manufacturers have realised this and can now put together a package of all the necessary bits and pieces with the necessary instructions. You need to look for the specialist shops and suppliers who advertise in the model boat magazines.

There are more complete kits available for fast electrics, and many of these even include the motor and a simple mechanical speed controller. They are also relatively inexpensive, and as only two-function radio is required, plus eight nickel cadmium fast recharge batteries for the power supply, fast electric racing at this level can be a

The Lesro Duplex RNLI Rigid Inflatable is all styrene moulded and although it is a bit of a squeeze to install the drive and ratio, it makes up into a real crowd-pulling and exciting model.

Several manufacturers supply grp hulls for a wide variety of scale craft from warships to tugs. A plan for scratchbuilding the rest of the model is supplied or can be purchased separately.

relatively cheap and quick way into power boat racing.

Again, up until fairly recently, the model yachtsman also purchased just the bare hull, usually in grp, and found out the rest the hard way. But now there are an increasing number of manufacturers who will supply a complete kit which only lacks the radio equipment. The yachting scene has probably also moved a stage further than all the other kit types as some manufacturers will supply a ready built model to order. You will find the small 575 at the local model shop and perhaps one of the one-designs, but it is unlikely that you will find the current competitive Marbleheads or 10rs. As with the power boats you will find one or two specialist shops but most model yacht manufacturers supply the customer direct. Again a look through the model magazines will highlight most of them.

Another different subject from the H.F.M. Marine boatyard is this electrically powered submersible, Deep Dive VI. It can run for up to 40 minutes on one charge and ideally requires 3-function radio, although operation is possible from 2-function. (Photo: Ray Brigden).

There are a number of yacht kits under 36in long available with styrene moulded hulls and decks and a working suit of sails.

Grading

Many manufacturers grade their kits in order of difficulty. Obviously what is difficult for one person is plain sailing (sorry) to another, but such systems do reduce the newcomer's bewilderment at the outset and should be accepted as a manufacturer's long term consideration of his customers. A very difficult expert's model might be a good sale, but if it puts that person off building another model the investment in the long term is nil.

Scratchbuilding really depends upon the availability of plans or the depth of research one is prepared to do. This SS *Great Britain* took two years to research and two years to build.

Scratchbuilding

The kit is certainly the most common way that most model boaters take up the hobby today. That was certainly not the case as little as ten years ago when most started off by building from a plan. The largest plans service in the world is based in this country and can offer thousands of designs covering everything from scale subjects to power to yacht, etc. There are also a number of smaller more specialised commercial suppliers. All produce catalogues of their designs and the first thing to do is to arm yourself with these listings.

Such plans can vary tremendously in quality and complexity. MAP, the supplier with the largest number of designs in their range, produce a star grading system, and most will be able to find something to their taste and experience within their range. The drawback is that for your specific combination of ability level and choice of design there will be a fairly limited range and the chosen model is likely to be a frequently modelled subject. This state of affairs may be of little consequence to some but very important to others who may wish to stand out from the crowd.

If you can't find your requirement from the commercial listings then unless you are very fortunate you must resign yourself to a long period of research. Some modellers find this a very rewarding part of building a model – others find it terribly frustrating. Obviously we are talking about a model of a prototype, hence somewhere sometime there were plans of that prototype drawn. Start with museums; the owners or

A scratchbuilt German model which features working fire monitors, crane, anchors, radar, lights and siren.

builders may still be in business; public libraries in port towns; commercial photographic archives; secondhand bookshops; etc. It is really detective work and can become quite absorbing.

For the power and yacht enthusiast there are again a large number of designs in the MAP range for most if not all of the categories raced, plus a very large number of freelance and sports models for the modeller who just wishes to build a vessel for Sunday afternoon sailing. Most of the power boat designs are for wood construction as grp moulding does not appeal to many modellers, although of course there is no reason why the person skilled in this material should not produce a wooden mould from the plans to form their own grp hull or hulls. Practically all of the yacht designs bar one or two assume that the modeller is experienced enough to build his yacht by whatever method he prefers, and hence only the bodylines, the shape of the boat at various positions along its length, are given together with a sailplan. There are however a couple of designs in the MAP range which do give more detailed practical building information particularly for new-comers.

Main construction methods

While the main aim of this book is to concentrate on the radio control aspect of model boating, at this point it would probably be of use to briefly discuss the main construction methods concerned with scratch-building wooden hulls. Once the basics are understood the reader will find a number of other books available commercially or at the public library which will expand on these aspects.

Boat hulls fall into two basic types, displacement and planing. The first type moves through the water whilst the second rides over the top. Displacement hulls are designed to offer as little resistance as possible to the water flowing past them and generate little if any upward lift. Design is always a compromise; the warship or liner is fast because of a long thin shape, but this can hardly be acceptable to a bulk carrier or oil tanker, hence the latter is fat and slow.

Planing hulls present an angled surface to the water and produce lift which raises the hull, reduces drag and allows the hull to move very fast for a relatively small increase in power.

Some designs automatically fall into one category or the other, but there are some shapes that can fit into either camp. A hard chine launch will act as a displacement model at low speeds but will climb onto its lower surfaces, if enough power is applied, and begin to plane. The hard chine refers to the point along the hull where the sides and bottoms meet at a sharp angle.

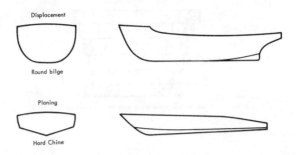

Displacement

Round bilge

Planing

Hard Chine

A hard chine hull is certainly the easiest type to model and should be a prime consideration for a beginner. It is also an inexpensive form of hull construction, requiring just a keel and formers, some stringers to act as chines and gunwales, and wooden skins for the sides, bottom and top. The design is excellent for power boats and practically all today's top racing designs in grp started life as a hard chine wooden boat.

Unfortunately the hard chine design is not so good for sailing craft, mainly because the boat is normally heeled over and the chines will create extra drag; however, it must be said that an absolute novice is still

This superb model of the Patrol Boat *Sri Kedah,* scratchbuilt by Gordon Lewis, won the National Championship for radio control scale ships in the early 1980s. (Photo by Ray Brigden).

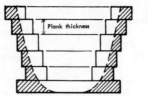

Deck level

Plank thickness

Section through Bread and Butter Hull Construction

recommended to go for one of the hard chine yacht designs which are easy to build and which also sail remarkably well, although not of course equable with a top sailing design.

A round bilge hull is therefore the normal choice for a sailing model. Equally unfortunately, round bilge hulls are not quite as straightforward as hard chine to construct. There are a number of methods of hull construction using wood; carved from the solid block; bread and butter or laminated block; composite; framed and planked. The former is seldom used for working models as it is expensive and hard work. Bread and butter which consists essentially of building up a block of the required size by gluing together layers of timber, usually in the form of planks of approximately 1in thickness, and then shaping the block to shape, is also less favoured today because of the cost of timber.

If the hull required is very boxy and only shows any shape at its extremities, a combination of bread and butter for the ends and a

An example of plank on frame construction which can be applied to any model with complex curvatures to its hull shape, in this instance a yacht.

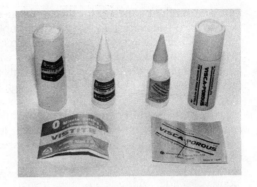

A selection of different viscosity cyanoacrylates, better known as 'Superglues', which are now available with gap filling properties and the ability to join porous materials such as balsa.

simple box section for amidships can work well. This system is known as composite.

The final method, which more closely follows the full-size method of construction than any of the others, is plank on frame. The method usually results in a lighter hull than would be achieved by the other methods and is most applicable to scale models with complex hull shapes and model yachts. However, practically any hull shape can be built using this method.

There are many other methods of hull construction used today, and particularly with functional competition models, heavy use is made of moulding techniques, producing glass reinforced plastic and/or styrene plastic hulls. However, the basic methods of wooden construction still hold true, because someone has to produce the original mould, and this is usually performed in wood.

Adhesives and finishing

A few words on these two subjects may be of help.

Few kits contain all necessary adhesives, but it is becoming increasingly common for the more unusual adhesives required, for instance, for the joining of ABS, to be included. If not included, manufacturers usually recommend the use of epoxy resin for plastic to plastic and plastic to wood joints. Epoxy can be used but it is certainly not the best for such materials. For ABS and styrene, ask your model shop to supply you with the correct liquid solvent. As well as using the solvent as recommended, it is a good idea to put a little solvent aside into a small jar and to add slivers of the plastic which will dissolve and create a thick gooey adhesive which can also be usefully employed as a filler.

If wood is to be stuck to plastic, try coating the wood with a thin film of the solvent or adhesive, allow to dry, and apply again to make the join. An excellent adhesive for this application is the liquid solvent sold in hardware stores for joining plastic drainpipe. It can be purchased in quite small tins which will last for many models.

For grp hulls, accessories can be fitted with epoxy resin or a better joint is obtained by using grp resin and glassfibre cloth. In both cases the surfaces to be mated should be roughened with a file or coarse glasspaper.

Scale models will need painting and while the hull and major areas can be finished off when assembled, it is usually much more convenient to paint small fittings before assembly. Matt paints are more realistic on scale models, and if they are given a thin covering of matt polyurethane varnish as a last coat, they will be more resistant to smudge marks from grease and slime. Many prefabricated kits, especially those using plastic components, are supplied with self-adhesive decals and do not require painting. Some of these are very long and difficult to apply correctly. Try wetting the model's surface with a soapy film, washing-up liquid is ideal, and you will find the decal can be slid around to the correct position. Allow to dry thoroughly. These decals do tend to make all the models look the same, though, and as plastic is much easier to paint than any wood surface, why not take advantage of that fact and make your model stand out from the crowd?

In conclusion

Whatever way you decide to start model boating – scratchbuilding or kits – do it now. Don't run away with the idea, though, that kits are only for beginners. Some kits are very sophisticated, complicated and challenging, producing exceptionally fine scale and functional models. Kits also give modellers the opportunity to tackle subjects that they might otherwise steer clear of. There is a wonderful world of variety awaiting. Why not take a look in your local model shop? You won't be disappointed.

Installations — in general   5

The arch enemy of radio control is water and dampness so obviously the model boating environment leaves a lot to be desired. The amazing thing is that most modellers treat their radio control equipment as though it can swim, and are most surprised when it fails to work one day. You wouldn't give your television or hi-fi a bath, would you? Radio control equipment does not ask for much today as regards its operating environment. It will stand incredible vibration – quite often being asked to work almost alongside an internal combustion engine revving at 20000rpm, or heat from a nearby exhaust system, and many other physical abuses. But it does not like water and in particular it positively loathes salt water. The problem with water and dampness, which after all is simply minute droplets of water in the air, is that the stuff conducts electricity if it is the slightest bit impure (and most ponds and lakes are very impure), and alters the electrical balance of circuits quite dramatically, usually to the extent where control of the model is lost. So in an ideal world the radio gear would be kept completely clear of all things damp and wet.

Unfortunately it isn't an ideal world so your radio will have to make the best of the conditions you provide for it. The good news is that there are many ways in which you can improve its lot and we will take a detailed look at all types of models further into this book. This chapter is simply to go over the ground rules, so to speak, and get you thinking as to how to make the most of a bad environment for your particular installation.

In many cases it is possible to install the complete radio gear in a watertight compartment or a watertight box within the model. The latter method has a number of advantages if you can manage it, not the least of which is the flexibility it gives you with other models. The same equipment can easily be moved from model to model with the minimum of disruption. In this arrangement it will be necessary for the radio box to be firmly fixed to the model, therefore the removal or isolation of the equipment from vibration must not be forgotten. The servos must be mounted using the rubber grommets that came with the

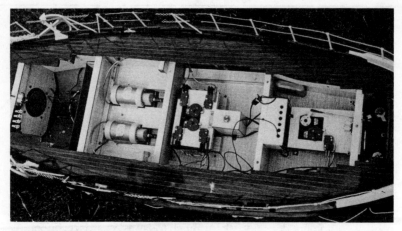

A neat and tidy installation in a lifeboat. Note how all the radio control equipment is mounted high and dry, clear of dripping hatch coamings, and conveniently sited.

radio – you didn't throw them away, did you? – and the receiver and batteries need to be settled into plastic foam beds.

Any wiring that has to exit the box can be led out through rubber grommets, whilst linkages from the servos to the operating surfaces can be led through suitable sized holes which can be protected by special commercial bellows or simply by the necks of party balloons suitably cut and held with rubber bands. Special output glands in metal or plastic can also be obtained, from specialist marine model shops, which do a similar job.

If this is to be your method, make sure that the box can be easily removed without having to take the deck off the model and that it is so positioned that nice, straight runs are available for the servo links to the

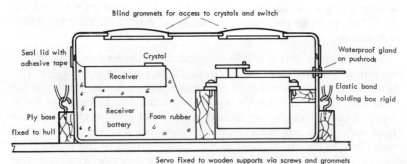

Section through Radio Box made from plastic lunch box

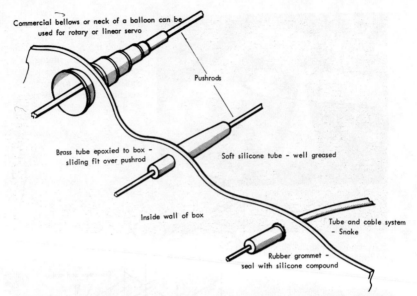

Commercial bellows or neck of a balloon can be used for rotary or linear servo

Pushrods

Brass tube epoxied to box - sliding fit over pushrod

Soft silicone tube - well greased

Inside wall of box

Tube and cable system - Snake

Rubber grommet - seal with silicone compound

rudder and engine, etc. Also obvious is the fact that the location needs to be the driest area of the model and as far away as feasible from any possible sources of radio interference such as powerful electric drive motors or spark ignition systems on some internal combustion engines. All these ifs and buts will contradict. The driest part of the boat, unless it's a yacht, will more than likely be at the bow or high in the superstructure, and these positions are in no way suitable when it comes to installing servo linkages. So there is a need to compromise.

A reasonable solution can be to locate the receiver and batteries in a watertight box, but to install the servos near to their work points. The

This receiver box from Robbe features a watertight rubber ring-sealed end cap and charging plugs. The aerial and servo leads are fed through a special opening which is highly water resistant if not waterproof.

Another example of high and dry radio gear mounting, although the receiver is a little too close to the coaming for comfort. Heavy electronic speed controller offset to match weight of receiver batteries.

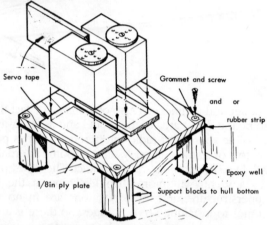

Servo tape

Grommet and screw

and   or

rubber strip

Epoxy well

1/8in ply plate

Support blocks to hull bottom

Again everything is mounted high and dry in this installation in a Clyde Puffer. The rudder servo is exactly in line with the rudder tiller and is firmly mounted using screws and anti-vibration grommets.

servos can be mounted on wooden bearers using the screws and grommets supplied with them, or perhaps stuck to a suitable surface with double-sided servo tape. The latter system must not be used for power boat models or the larger yachts as the forces applied to the servos can be quite considerable. If they have to be mounted in a wet area, and there are few places on a boat that are not wet, then mount them as high as possible and not directly under hatch coamings which are a favourite place for drips to enter.

Rudder posts are another favourite place for water ingress, especially if the top of the rudder is below the water level of the model. Some servos are now available in a waterproofed condition. They are especially sealed at the factory and will withstand the most severe dunkings, but they are expensive. A reasonable degree of watertightness can be achieved by carefully loosening the screws which hold the servo together and smearing the adjoining case edges with Vaseline or silicone grease or even a thin film of contact adhesive. The latter method is not as drastic as it sounds as the adhesive will easily peel away for future access and it is not greasy like the other methods. If servos are located some distance from the rest of the equipment, make sure that wiring is supported and not allowed to hang free.

A suitable area can usually be found quite easily in a scale boat, especially one that is electric powered. However, a steam powered

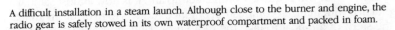

A difficult installation in a steam launch. Although close to the burner and engine, the radio gear is safely stowed in its own waterproof compartment and packed in foam.

All radio equipment is installed in a watertight compartment which itself is a permanent fixture in this yacht hull. Note raised hatch coaming which can be packed with silicone grease before firmly fitting the hatch.

model will require a special compartment for the radio installation. Dampness mixed with the heat and humidity of a steam plant is about the worst combination you can get, short of the leaky submarine model! A power boat will require a similar set-up and it is now almost standard practice with internal combustion engined models to provide an area at the stern of the boat to take the radio gear. Until a few years ago most modellers would create a waterproof compartment at the rear of the model by installing a bulkhead and boxing in the entire compartment with a sealed clear plastic lid which enabled one to check that the compartment was still dry. There are now a number of purpose-designed radio boxes that can be installed as a permanent part of the boat and they come complete with linkage outlet glands, grommets, switch and crystal access points and usually a special rubber lip for the clear plastic cover.

The positioning of the box in a yacht is quite important and as near to the centre of gravity as possible is the ideal location so that the weight has little or no effect on the handling of the model. It is more than likely that the servo will have to be mounted outside the box, otherwise long linkages are required and these can cause sloppy control problems, and almost inevitable that the sail winch is mounted separately. Water ingress is a greater problem with a yacht than any other model boat as its deck will spend much of its time awash even in relatively calm conditions.

Fast electric models are another special case as they are usually much too small for a box installation to be acceptable, and furthermore weight is a very important consideration in a racing electric model. The accepted method, and it certainly isn't ideal, but no-one has as yet come up with a better alternative, is to put the receiver into a polyurethane bag and seal it as best as possible with freezer tape or Sellotape. Freezer tape is better as it remains sticky under cold and wet conditions as opposed to ordinary Sellotape which loses its effectiveness once damp. A small bag of a chemical called silica gel, which can be obtained from most chemists, can be included in the polythene bag. Silica gel absorbs large quantities of water for its own equivalent weight and will stop condensation forming in the bag when the outside temperature and humidity change. It is important, though, that the bag is regularly taken out and dried over a radiator or similar heat source. The servos will have to take their chances, but sealing them as mentioned will help.

Don't forget when siting your radio box or receiver bag that you may require quick access to change crystals. With the polythene bag job you have no option but to start again with a fresh bag, but with the radio box a large hole can be shaped at a suitable point over the crystal socket and sealed with a large rubber blank obtained from motor car accessory shops. The same method can be used for access to on/off switches and charging sockets.

Aerials can be a problem, especially with scale models. However, unless you intend to sail out of sight, the modern radio receiver will be

A typical installation in a fast electric model. Shortage of room usually necessitates a compromise and the gear has to be fitted in available spaces, hence it is important that the deck hatch be made as watertight as possible.

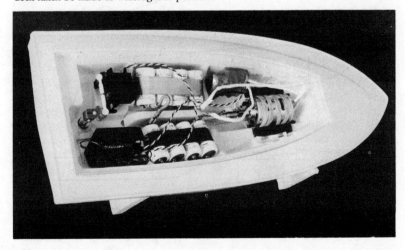

able to function entirely satisfactorily with the aerial mounted below deck. It can be routed under the deck and held in place with sticky tape. Alternatively it could be run up the inside of a mast or hidden in a part of the superstructure.

Power boats and yachts will travel much greater distances away from the transmitter and will also be operating in conjunction with at least five other models and sometimes as many as eleven others. It is important therefore that the best possible reception conditions are provided on the model. A power boat can have a metal whip aerial of approximately 15in height and this can be scratchbuilt from piano wire or it can be one of the commercial products now available. The model yacht can also use a whip aerial, or advantage can be taken of the shrouds which support the mast to support the aerial or even to double as the aerial. In the latter case some precautions have to be taken to ensure the aerial is at the correct length, which will be covered in detail later.

Batteries for the receiver will normally be installed close to it. If your equipment uses replaceable dry cells then obviously there must be a reasonable access in spite of the precautions taken to keep the water out. Dry cells do not last for many outings and will require replacement frequently. If rechargeable cells are used the same requirements apply in that the cells will need to be removed or at the least accessed for

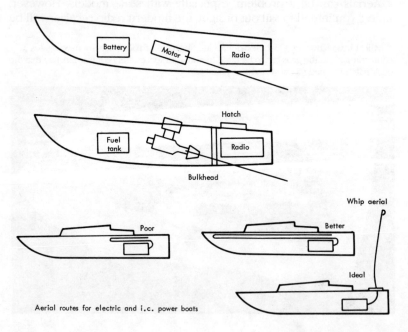

Aerial routes for electric and i.c. power boats

water tight output bushing

Commercial waterproof output bushings consisting of plastic square bars sliding in bushes located in bulkheads and secured with circlips. The sliding bars contain three grooves filled with grease to facilitate water repulsion.

connection to a charger after every outing. However, radio equipment which incorporated rechargeable cells when purchased will almost certainly have a charging socket fitted into the switch harness and a corresponding matching plug from a suitable charger. This system is very convenient, sometimes too convenient as it is easy to neglect carrying out a regular inspection of the radio box for water ingress.

Corrosion of battery cell cases can occur, or more likely will be corrosion of the wiring harness. There is a particular problem with the negative leads of the battery supply which need regular inspection. For a complicated chemical reason, the negative lead corrodes at a greater rate than the positive lead in any circuit fed by a battery, and this rate of decay appears to increase markedly in damp conditions. The moral is inspect regularly, at least monthly and more frequently in models prone to wetness, such as multi-race boats and yachts.

If you have the misfortune, or even desire if you are an off-shore enthusiast, to operate in salt water, it is even more essential that every drop of salt water is kept well away from radio control equipment. Indeed should you be unfortunate enough to get salt water into your equipment, receiver or servos, then the best immediate procedure is to wash it out with copious amounts of fresh water and then begin the drying out procedure.

So in conclusion to our chapter which takes an overall look at installations, the over-riding factor controlling a radio installation in a model boat must be that all aims should be towards keeping water away and the equipment dry.

6 Installations in scale model boats

In chapter five we emphasised a number of times the need to keep water away from radio equipment and also suggested briefly some different methods to achieve this desirable state of affairs. Except for very small models and special cases such as submarines, there will be enough room in any scale model to accommodate a variety of methods.

The lunch-box

Most modellers will have more than one scale model and hence the radio gear will need to be installed in a manner which allows for relatively quick removal and reinstallation, and yet when *in situ* is rigidly positioned to facilitate precise control movement. The 'lunch-box' system is very suitable, so-called because for the many years before commercial radio compartments came on the scene, most modellers made use of the plastic 'lunch-box' containers available in most chain stores and supermarkets. There was initially only a limited range of these containers on the market, but with the advent of home freezers there is now a very large range of containers in all shapes and sizes, and it should not prove too difficult to find one to fit the space available in your model. The material of construction is usually polythene and it is almost impossible to find an adhesive that will work with this plastic, therefore you will have to resort to physical fixing methods such as bolts and screws.

Only the servos will need positive fixing to either the sides or bottom of the box. With a 'lunch-box', the bottom will probably be more substantial. The commercial boxes are usually moulded from a more suitable and usually more rigid plastic – sometimes glass reinforced plastic is used and this type is even easier to fix bearers etc. to as epoxy resin can be used. But back to the 'lunch-box' arrangement. One quick method which will be entirely suitable for all electric powered scale models is to use double-sided adhesive servo tape which can be purchased from most model shops or radio accessory outlets. This is a

An eggbox construction which provides ready-made compartments for radio gear. However, in a small high speed model such as this a waterproof box would have been better.

tape approximately 1 to 2mm thick and 15 to 20mm wide in lengths varying from 25mm to 150mm. Each side is coated with a strong adhesive protected until use with special plastic film. On removal of this film the tape is first stuck to the servo, which should then be carefully positioned, because you only get one go, and stuck into its correct location in the box after removal of the other piece of film. If the workshop or workroom is cold, you may find the adhesive is not very sticky. A little warmth applied from a fan heater or other convenient source will bring the 'stickiness' back. If you have inadvertently stuck the servo in the wrong place, servo tape which refuses to lift from a surface can be dissolved away by the careful application of a little paint thinners on a paper towel or rag.

For real security wooden bearers can be fixed to the bottom of the box using woodscrews driven through from underneath. An alternative method is to fix wooden rails along the sides of the box; 6 × 6mm strip will suffice. When you purchased your radio equipment there would have been a small accessory pack containing some small screws, washers and rubber grommets. The rubber grommets should be inserted into the servo mounting lug holes and the screws inserted through these into the wooden bearers. Do not overtighten. It is important that a small amount of flexibility is retained to absorb shocks and vibration.

Again, the 'lunch-box' will probably need strengthening . One way of achieving this is to fix a plywood plate into the bottom of the box with small screws.

The receiver can either be wrapped in a strip of foam or positioned in a foam bed shaped from a suitable sized piece, or again servo tape can be used to stick the receiver to an adjacent surface. The last method is best used if you will require to gain access to the crystal socket without taking the lid off the container. A relatively firm support to the receiver will be required to accommodate the minimal but relatively firm force required to remove and replace a crystal. Large rubber blanking plugs up to 40mm diameter can be obtained from motor accessory shops and all that is required is that a suitably sized hole, just smaller than the plug diameter, be cut in the top or side of the box in order that once the plug is removed, the crystal can be accessed. The battery pack can be treated similarly to the receiver and either stuck or embedded in foam.

Switches are prime areas of trouble when they get damp or wet, so while these can be mounted on the surface of the box, it is a much better idea to site them close to the crystal plug which can then be used for two purposes – switching on/off and changing frequencies. With models carrying a large amount of rigging and complicated or delicate superstructures, it can sometimes be difficult or at the least a time-consuming task to gain access inside the model. The switch can be mounted remote from the receiver – if necessary the wires can be extended by soldering or a purchased extension lead which has a plug on one end and a socket on the other can be fitted. The switch can then be hidden under a deckhouse, hatch, or similar disguised position. One modeller always hides his switches under an upturned bucket! If you do

Special models demand special techniques; this model of the first submersible, the one-man operated and powered *Turtle,* uses the whole bottom of the model as a watertight compartment for drive and radio gear.

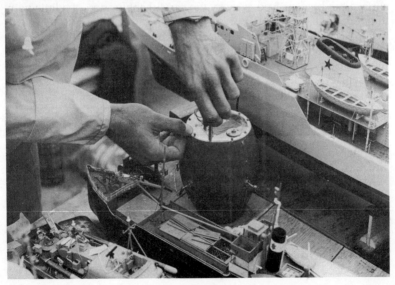

84

use this system, it is even more important that you do not neglect the regular inspection for corrosion and damp.

Back at the 'lunch-box', holes will also be required for the aerial and any servo linkages. The aerial requirement is relatively straightforward and a small rubber grommet will usually suffice to bring out the wire. This can be sealed with a smear of silicone grease and led away to be taped under the deck or up a mast.

Servo linkages are a bit more difficult to handle but not impossible. For many years linear servos made the job relatively straightforward. These are servos which give their output as a pure push/pull motion along one axis rather than the rotary type which suffer from a sideways displacement as the servo disc rotates. Unfortunately linear servos are now almost extinct.

A slot is therefore needed in the side of the box and this is a little more difficult to seal. The generally accepted method is to cut the neck from a party balloon and trap the wide end against the outside of the box with a large washer – the fibre kind sold in motor accessory shops are ideal. This will need trimming with a slot and fixing to the side of the box can be achieved with a number of small bolts and nuts. The other end of the balloon surrounds the wire pushrod and is sealed against it with rubber bands or a small cable tie. The latter is another relatively new product made for the electrical industry. It consists of a plastic strip with small teeth and it can be formed into a loop and closed upon itself by pulling the free end. Once clamped around something it cannot be released without cutting free. They are available in a range of sizes and are very cheap – try the local High Street electrical component shop. There is a nationwide American based chain in the UK whose shops are like Aladdin's caves for radio control modellers.

Most model shops will stock rubber gaiters or bellows which will do the same job with a little less trouble. They will have a hole at one end to accept the wire link and a lipped opening at their large end to push through a suitably sized hole.

An alternative method is to use a 'Z' crank through a bush in the top or side of the box, but this system introduces a number of extra pivot points in the system and can easily result in sloppy linkages. Snakes, or a cable running wihin a close-fitting tube can also be used, but these systems are much more suited to power boat installations and will be dealt with in more detail in the relevant chapter.

If the box is to be removable then a positive location will be required so that it always drops back into the correct location. A favourite method is to fix four blocks to a mounting tray to locate the box, which can then be simply held *in situ* by rubber bands stretched over and secured to screw hooks fitted to the mounting tray. The tray can be cut from 2mm plywood and mounted clear of the bottom of the model by

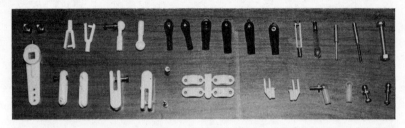

Just a small example of the incredibly wide range of clevises and links currently available at most model shops.

wooden bearers, or strung between convenient bulkheads or frames.

Before we leave the subject of the radio box or compartment, don't forget the handy tip concerning the silica gel bag mentioned in a previous chapter. This chemical will absorb many times its own weight in water and has a great affinity for the wet stuff. It can be purchased from chemists and should be fed into small linen bags about 30 × 30mm sewn closed at the top. Place the bags over a radiator or a similar hot source for a couple of hours to drive out any moisture and then place the bag in the radio box. At the end of the sailing session remove the bag and redry as above. This system is especially good at keeping condensation at bay, a problem that frequently occurs if the radio is sealed at home in a warm room and then submitted to the damp environment in the vicinity of cold water.

Separate servos

Sometimes it will be more convenient to have the servos mounted separately from the receiver box, especially where small models are concerned and there is simply not enough room for a combined receiver, battery and servos package. The receiver and batteries can still be treated to the box system – indeed it will be much easier because there will be no linkage problem and only outlets for aerial and servo wires will be called for, which can pass through grommets and be sealed with grease as before.

The servos can be positioned adjacent to the surface which they have to control and should be mounted either on wooden bearers as for the box installation discussed earlier, or on a proprietary servo mounting tray or a plywood tray. Again, don't forget the vibration/shock absorbing grommets. This is the simplest method of installation but certainly not the best. It will work for most models but however well you site the servos away from hatch edges and points where water is likely to enter the hull, the day will inevitably come when the wet stuff wins! It is far

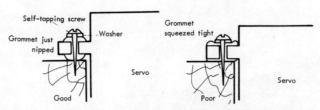

better practice to locate all the radio components together in a watertight box or compartment.

The compartments idea is more suited to power boat models but can be worthwhile for 'fast' scale models and special models such as submarines. The system incorporates a section of the model as a completely enclosed watertight compartment in which all the radio equipment is located. We will take a much closer look when we come to discuss power boat installations.

Linkages

Linkages for scale models will in most instances be only applicable to the rudder. Speed control will be electronic, or if mechanical only a very short linkage will be required. There is an enormous range of fittings and clevises available today which will create some confusion among newcomers.

First it must be said that the biggest failing of most radio control modellers is sloppy linkages. The precision and efficient operation of the whole system is often spoilt by neglecting a part of the installation which will cost something less than 2% of the total expenditure on the entire model.

From inspection of many models experiencing radio gear failure or inaccurate control, it is apparent that the most common cause can be traced to bad design and/or installation of the mechanical connections or linkages between servos and operating surfaces.

Today's servos are marvellous examples of precision engineering and involve some of the most modern techniques to give you a strong, reliable mechanism capable of giving accurate resolution of control signals to tolerances below 1%. It is an insult to this technology and a waste of money to use a bent piece of wire and mutilate the servo arms to achieve a solid, tight linkage that immediately removes any possibility of achieving the wonderfully accurate control that is offered by all modern proportional radio control systems.

There is only one over-riding factor with regard to the subject of servo linkages. A servo should never be forced to overload or stall by tight linkages, rudder posts, throttle arms, etc. Everything should be

87

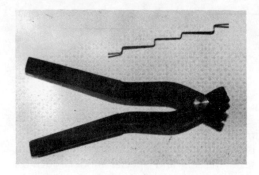

The Z bender is a unique and very useful tool for bending Z shaped ends to piano wire to make servo links. Available at most model shops.

precise yet free to move easily. We have already mentioned snakes and these will be discussed in detail when we come to look at power boats. The system used almost universally by scale models is known as pushrod.

Pushrod

The best system in any mechanical set-up is usually the simplest method that will achieve the desired objective. The pushrod certainly falls into this category. Pushrods for model boat use are not required to be light, as are those for model aircraft which use lightweight balsa and wire, but can be constructed from wire rod universally obtainable. 16swg (1.5mm) is about the right size (some modellers use bicycle spokes), or they can also be purchased commercially produced from model shops. These usually have one or both ends screwed to accept an adjustable clevis, a springy piece of forked metal or a plastic moulding which clips onto the servo arm or rudder linkage through suitably drilled holes, and which is threaded on the other end to screw onto the wire rod and give the facility of adjusting the length of the linkage. This adjustment will allow for final precise setting of the linkage in case of slight errors when positioning the servo.

Home-made pushrods can be produced by simply bending to the Z shape on their ends as shown in the figures. This can be achieved by

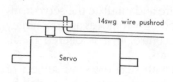

14swg wire pushrod

Servo

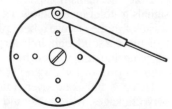

Servo disc cut away to prevent fouling clevis

careful use of thin long-nosed pliers if such a tool is already in your toolbox. If not you would be well advised to purchase a neat tool which will easily form the bends for you and provide a wire cutting facility also. Washers are not normally needed if this tool is used as sharp bends are formed, but if you are using pliers it is not easy to obtain a sharp radius on the bends and the washers will prevent binding on the output disc or arm in these circumstances.

An alternative to the Z shape is to simply bend the wire into the L shape shown. To prevent the linkage working free it is necessary to remove the servo disc and to mount the L pin facing upwards. This method will only work on rotary discs where the servo top prevents dropout. A better solution which will work on all output arms is to solder on a thin keeper wire to pass under the disc or purchase special plastic keepers which do the same job.

We have already mentioned commercial clevises and the screwed ends can be purchased for fitting into your own wire links, although an 8BA threading die will be required to thread 14swg rod. Alternatively there is an adaptor which can be soldered onto wire rod and a clevis is then screwed onto the exposed threaded end of the adaptor. There is an incredibly wide selection of commercial accessories in this area – it is practically an industry in its own right – and a few minutes spent in your local model shop taking stock of what's available would be time well spent.

An unfortunate problem with clevises as opposed to Z and L links is the possibility of the forks of the clevis jamming on the edge of the output disc. This is not so much a problem with straight arms and linear servos. So, during the set-up period and testing, operate the servo through maximum throw plus trim to ensure that this problem does not occur. It may be necessary to cut away part of the disc as shown.

All clevises which rely on the fork principle can obviously jam the servo operation should the radio system become unstable – e.g. in the

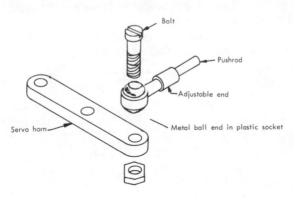

case of bad interference – and this stalled condition can cause major damage to the servo amplifier components.

This can be totally avoided by using the ball and socket system. The metal ball is screwed into the output arm and held in place by a locking nut. The plastic socket is a push fit over the ball and once in place it is capable of being rotated through any horizontal and limited vertical angles with no binding or slop.

Equal or unequal movement

Ensure that the angles between the rudder arm and the linkage and the linkage and the servo disc, or arm, are at right angles, to ensure equal control surface movements. This will also prevent the situation arising where the extreme control surface arm position, particularly rudder, together with any inherent play in the linkage, may allow the arm to flip over beyond the point-of-no-return position. A frequent cause of excess play, especially in lightweight glass reinforced plastic or styrene scale hulls, is the flexible nature of the hull, allowing movement at the top of the rudder post. This can be prevented by fixing a substantial wooden block across the bottom of the hull or by using a support connected to the transom or a bulkhead adjacent to the top of the tube.

During the pre-installation testing stage to determine linkage positions and lengths, you would have checked the servo movements to make sure that they operated in the correct sense, i.e., left on the rudder stick causes the model to steer to the left, and that the amount of movement given at the control surface would not be too large or too small for the desired effect.

If the sense is incorrect you can change to the other side of the disc although this can give unfavourable linkage geometry, or it may be more desirable to reverse the direction of the servo. A few years ago this could only be achieved by purchasing an additional electronic accessory and these are still available. However, if buying your servos separately they can be specified in right or left handed forms, and furthermore many transmitters now include small switches which will carry out this change at the flick of the switch.

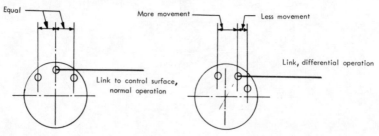

To obtain equal movement of control surface arm as compared to servo output arm, the radii of the disc and control surface arm must be identical. Extended arms can be purchased for servos giving a greater movement at the control surface, or by also extending the control surface arm, if the same freedom of fit is involved as on the shorter arms, then the whole system will incorporate a relatively lower freedom (slop) factor. By the way, most rudders are at their maximum efficiency up to 25 degrees either side of neutral. Going over this simply turns the rudder into a brake and puts extra loads on the servo.

Occasions arise when unequal control surface movements are desirable, i.e., a model which turns more one way than the other, and the figure explains the theory behind differential linkages.

Closed loop

In this system the servo pushes and pulls at the same time. This prevents the side and bending force on a link and is particularly suited for systems where large power requirements are called for, for instance the rudder on a radio controlled hydroplane – see later. It can be of benefit in certain scale models though, particularly older ships whose rudder chains or cables travelled through runners or pulleys along each side of the wheelhouse and/or bulwarks from the wheel to the rudder capstan. Typical ships using this method were Clyde Puffers and tugs. The lines can be of terylene or nylon and allowed to change direction over polished wire guides or pulleys or rings.

Linkage hints

If you need to operate a twin rudder installation, this can be achieved by using a bellcrank fitted to one rudder, with its fore and aft arm linked to a fore and aft tiller on the other. The arm lengths of the bellcrank can

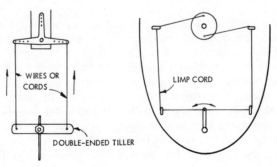

This installation in the stern of a steam launch uses the closed loop system of control which is extremely positive and kind on the servo output shaft bearings.

also be altered to provide differential movement if required. Remember that the bellcrank will reverse the mode of operation.

To join wire rods without access to soldering equipment, use the metal centres of so-called 'chocolate blocks' or electrical wiring terminal blocks.

Piano wire that breaks on bending needs annealing. This can be accomplished by heating to red heat and allowing to cool slowly.

Metal to metal joints should be avoided since they can produce electrical interference with radio reception, although modern equipment is unlikely to suffer from such problems. If in any doubt, use a plastic clevis.

Aerial

There are a number of small but important details to be considered. First of all an inside aerial should enable a range of at least 80 metres which should be ample for all scale models.

Make sure when routing the aerial wire away from the receiver box that it does not run parallel to any other wiring and keep it away from the drive motor or motors and associated wiring. Do not alter the total length of the wire. This is especially important if a disguised aerial is used. This can be hidden in the rigging, especially with warships. Even ships' railings could be utilised but the total length of the aerial must not exceed the length of the original wire connected to the receiver when purchased. The length of the scale aerial must be removed from the aerial wire attached to the receiver before joining the disguised part of the aerial and the remaining receiver part together.

Steam models

Most of the foregoing applies to steam powered models; however, these craft do provide the worst possible conditions of not only dampness, but also heat. It is almost mandatory for a separate sealed compartment to be provided and the servos should be of the waterproofed type or sealed with silicone grease or contact adhesive as mentioned previously. If a complete compartment or part of the boat is made for the radio equipment, the compartment must be sealed off from the rest of the model by bulkheads glued or resined into position. The resulting box can then be rimmed with 10 or 15mm square wooden strips. This coaming must be sanded or filed flat. The hatch cover should be constructed from Perspex or acrylic sheet which can be obtained from hardware merchants. Thicknesses of from 3 to 5mm are acceptable. Drill clearance holes around the edge of the sheet, at approximately 50mm centres, to accommodate ⅝in by No. 8 self tapping screws. Use the cover as a template and drill ³⁄₃₂in diameter holes in the wood coaming and carefully drive the screws home. When fitting the cover during normal use, smear a thin film of silicone grease over the coaming and as the hatch is screwed down and the surfaces come together, a clear indication of a good seal is apparent. An alternative to grease is to shape and fit a thin rubber sealing gasket. Some model shops now sell rubber strip with adhesive on one side purely for this task. The object of the transparent hatch cover, of course, is to enable a visual inspection to be carried out for water ingress.

Servo installation in a confined space using a sheet metal prefabrication as servo holder. The servo is switching a mechanical switcher.

Submarines and low freeboard models

Everyone knows what a submarine is, but what is a low freeboard model? There has been a trend over recent years towards smaller models, which in itself creates problems in keeping dry as obviously the small model still has to work in full-size waves. Often these small models are almost awash and require submarine techniques as far as installation is concerned. A typical boat in this category was the *Monitor*, an armour-plated hull, absolutely flat and with a freeboard of less than 3ft – at 1:96 scale that's just 0.375in – which fought in the American Civil War.

The method used with these types of models demands a similar approach to the enclosed compartment system described above for steam powered models, except that in these instances the whole of the engine compartment and radio area is constructed as a complete watertight container. This can be achieved using the same method of forming a relatively substantial lip around the whole of the compartmentalised area and screwing down a transparent hatch, although in these instances it will be necessary to have the screws spaced closer together, say 30mm centres, and the plastic to be at least 5mm thick.

A few strokes of a bicycle pump through a tyre valve fitted to a watertight compartment will provide slight positive pressure tending to prevent water entry along prop-shafts etc. Submersible on the right has a silicone rubber bed (DIY bath sealant) moulded to the hatch shape during construction, the hatch being screwed down on it in use.

A positive seal achieved by a wide coaming strip, itself bedded on silicone, with the hatch/superstructure nutted down.

Below, the submarine-type radio compartment as a watertight container extending over most of the hull is effective for low freeboards: the deck is awash on this model. (Photo Ray Brigden).

Some modellers create a slightly positive pressure within this area as an extra precaution. If the interior pressure can be maintained at even just a fraction above the outside ambient pressure, air will always be trying to move from the compartment to outside and will tend to prevent water seeping in through rudder posts, linkage outlets, propeller shafts, etc.

This desirable state of affairs can be achieved by installing a car type valve into the hatch cover. This can be obtained from an old inner tube and either screwed into position if you have the correct threading equipment, or just as effectively fixed with cyanoacrylate adhesive (Superglue). A bicycle pump is then connected to the valve and very gentle pressure applied until resistance is felt on the pump. Don't overdo the pumping or the system will not work at all.

7 Installations in racing boats

For internal combustion engined power boats used for racing the position of radio control equipment is today almost standardised at the rear of the model. The main reason for this is that races have become longer over the years – 30 minutes is now the norm and many races are for 1 hour. The fuel requirement for a 30 minute race can be carried on board, but only if practically all the centre section of the boat is given over to fuel tank space. The centre of gravity needs to be approximately 40% of the length of the boat measured from the transom. The fuel tank must sit as near as possible to this point so that the centre of gravity is not affected as the fuel load lightens. The engine, being the next heaviest mass, will need to be placed just forward of the C/G, and so the radio position is rather forced upon one. Next to the transom might seem ideal inasmuch as the rudder servo is only going to need a short linkage, although of course the throttle linkage is going to be difficult, particularly with the large tank in the way, but also the area is the wettest place in the boat. Obviously therefore it is imperative that

A typical multi-boat layout with radio hatch at the rear, featuring four screws to hold down the hatch under all hazardous conditions.

whatever method of radio installation is chosen it must be absolutely watertight.

Compartmentalised

In view of these requirements most modellers today use the watertight compartment method: that is, the whole of the rear of the boat is used for radio installation and is constructed as a watertight chamber. This is relatively straightforward and can be accomplished as described in the chapter covering scale boat installations with reference to steam powered models. The compartment is sealed off with suitable bulkheads and a transparent hatch fitted onto perfectly smooth coamings. The bulkheads can be of 2mm plywood or even thick card reinforced with glass fibre resin and mat. Simply cut them roughly to shape and fix temporarily into position with five-minute epoxy, then reinforce the edges and corners with 25mm wide strips of glassfibre mat and apply resin. When dry the whole area can be coated with one of the proprietary coloured resin glazing products obtainable from model shops. The hatch and seal should be constructed as per the instructions given in chapter six.

The disadvantage with this method is that it takes a relatively long time to gain access to the radio equipment at the pondside, but surely this is a small price to pay for peace of mind concerning the security of your radio system.

A number of commercial radio boxes specifically designed for this type of installation can now be purchased. These are simply resined

Tried and trusted for 18 years, a hatch screwing down onto silicone greased coamings works well. Today's sophisticated radio boxes are natural developments of this system. The large rubber blanking plug allows access for switching on/off.

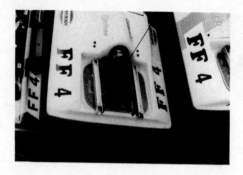

Two metal rails hinged at one end and screwed at the other to allow quicker access to the compartment is a comparatively recent innovation.

into the rear of the model and sealed at their tops and edges to form in effect a rear compartment. The advantage over scratchbulding is that these kits contain all the necessary bits and pieces such as bellows, charging sockets, rubber lip seal, special watertight switches and aerial outlets, etc. They also now feature a quick method of access whereby the hatch is held down by two angled strips of aluminium alloy, hinged at one end, and secured at the other with a screw or clamping bolt. This method can also be home-made with a little care, needing perhaps a modicum of more precise engineering skill than is necessary with the multi-screw system.

The sports boat

For the sports boat or launch which will not need to carry such a large quantity of fuel, there will be enough room to mount the radio in any convenient spot that is high and dry. A favourite trick, not seen so often these days, was to suspend the radio box from four springs, one at each corner, back to mounting points under the deck. Obviously, only the receiver and batteries can be accommodated in the box in this type of installation.

Fixing the box

An alternative method of fixing the box is to install a frame on the hull bottom and sit the radio box within the frame, holding it in place with strong rubber bands. With glass reinforced plastic hulls simply sit the box in the hull at the correct location and mark the position of the four corners on the hull bottom. Roughen this area with coarse glasspaper and then smear a little Vaseline or silicone grease on the bottom of the

This commercial compartment is resined into the boat and the seal is a rubber strip. The receiver etc., is packed in foam to absorb vibration. (Photo Pete Dirs).

radio box at its four corners. This is to act as a release agent for resin based filler or Plastic Padding, a mixture of glass reinforced resin and an inert filler to stop it running. Prepare enough of this material to form a pad at each corner of the radio box. Apply onto the hull bottom at the marked points and then gently press the radio box with its four greased corners into the resin filler. Leave until set, usually around 20 to 30 minutes, and then ease the box away from the pads, whereupon four pads with matching indentations to the bottom corners of the radio box will ensure that it always reseats into exactly the same spot following maintenance or use in another model. Again, strong rubber bands will hold the box in place.

All radio gear is enclosed in this long compartment in this American hydroplane. Servo discs protrude through silicone sealed holes. The whole box can be removed by simply releasing the L shaped bracket mounted on the rear engine bulkhead.

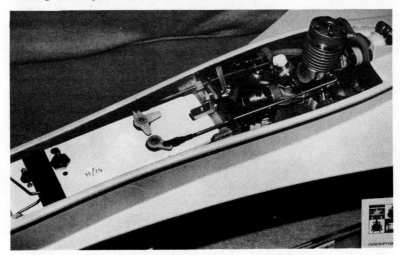

Fast electric models never have enough room to include radio boxes or compartments and usually the best has to be made of a bad job. Extra maintenance after every outing is demanded.

Fast electric models

In the late 60s a number of modellers took one or two models designed for internal combustion power and built them very light with balsa wood. These designs were available in plan form through the model magazines and more and more modellers became interested in this quiet form of racing models. The main drawback was the weight and inability of the lead acid cells to accept a quick charge, and the lack of suitable motors.

The breakthrough came in the 70s with the advent of cheap fast rechargeable nickel cadmium cells and motors designed for marine use. The motors were American, yet only the British were to see the immediate potential of combining these two new technologies. In the summer of 1971 at the European Model Power Boat Championships, hosted by NAVIGA in Belgium, British modellers took Gold and Silver

A high speed commercial mass produced fast electric kit from West Germany featuring two powerful motors driving a surface piercing propeller through a gearbox, powered by nicad cells.

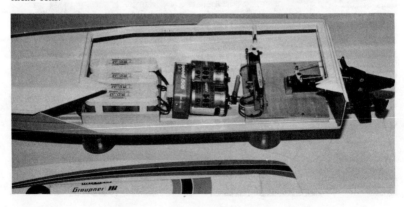

The two most popular motors throughout the world for fast electrics; the Mabuchi 540 and smaller 380. Right, a high performance British electric motor featuring multi-pole commutator and special rare earth magnets which give a very high efficiency figure.

medals and placed Great Britain at the forefront of 'fast electrics', a position held for the next decade.

Unfortunately the American, and later German, specialist fast electric motors were expensive, and many were deterred from moving into this side of our hobby. It was the Germans and Japanese who created the next breakthrough with ultra cheap motors. The German motor was a small industrial motor, unfortunately no longer available, which gave a performance comparable with a 3.5cc internal combustion engine, while the Japanese motors were initially developed for the rapidly growing 1:12 scale radio control car market.

The introduction of the 'Restricted' formula, which limits competitors to using a standard off-the-shelf motor and 8 off 1.2 volt, 1.2 ampere/hour nickel cadmium cells, allows for modellers to experiment with their own designs or to use either the specialist hulls manufactured for this class or even one of the many kits originally designed for sports racing, but many of which are very competitive in this category.

Internal combustion powered models have their radio installations influenced by the position of the fuel tank. Similarly, fast electrics have theirs dictated by the drive battery location. There are two basic methods of installing the drive cells: in two separate packs along the sides of the model with the radio equipment in between or with the cells as a complete block, similar to the fuel tank in the i.c. boat. No matter what system is used, it is practically always impossible to find room for a separate radio box installation. The aim with all fast electric boats is to keep the weight and size as low as possible for a given amount of power. These constraints demand that the receiver and servos will have to operate in undesirable conditions, but this is the price one has to pay for a competitive performance with a fast electric model. The sports enthusiast may be able to find enough space to incorporate a receiver and battery box, but the servos will need to be mounted separately.

Fortunately most modern servos are quite robust and in some instances water resistant. Note water resistant, not waterproof – there is a world of difference. Many suppliers produce a plastic moulded servo tray which is a very neat way of mounting servos. Unfortunately they are also rather heavy. A much better alternative, originally put forward by one of the UK's leading fast electric exponents for many years, is constructed from thin aluminium sheet as per the figure. Cut a piece of plate 140 × 30mm. Take the servo and measure its base length and width plus the distance from the base to the support lugs. Add 2mm to these dimensions to form the clearance for fixing into the hull, allowing sufficient overhang on the section in which to seat and support the servo. Drill the correct sizes and positioned holes in the overhanging parts to accept the servo fixing self tapping screws, not forgetting the rubber grommets. Bend to shape and fit the servo. The resulting unit will suit all the larger fast electric models and can also be used for i.c. boats if necessary.

With the smaller less powerful models, double-sided servo tape installations can be used, as per scale models, but it must be realised that an impact with another model or the bank is quite likely to break the joint with disastrous consequences.

The general fate of the receiver is the polythene bag wrapped in foam to insulate from mechanical vibration and jolts. Regular inspection is a necessity, ideally after every day's outing.

Servo strength

For all but the most powerful engines, or models which do not feature a balanced rudder, the standard servo as supplied with the original equipment will be completely satisfactory. It is highly unlikely that a

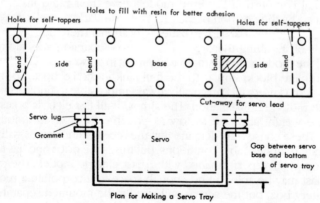

Plan for Making a Servo Tray

model cannot be trimmed to operate with a balanced rudder, which is to be much preferred because it reduces the load on the servo which provides mechanical and electrical benefits – as well as prolonging the life of the servo.

Rudders

Balancing a rudder is simply a matter of positioning the hinge line back from the leading edge so that part of the rudder is in front of this line and part behind. When the rudder is operated, the impinging water stream on the front part helps to turn the rudder and once held in the turned position it continues to relieve the servo of the necessary forces that would otherwise be required to hold the position. A perfect balance is not required, hence only the most extreme cases will not have some degree of balancing.

One such type is the radio controlled hydroplane, which by virtue of its design, has a completely non-balanced rudder. A standard servo will be able to cope with 3.5cc powered boats, although it will probably need a closed loop system, see later. However, larger engined models will need a more powerful servo as well. These are available separately and some include ball-raced output arms as an added refinement.

Powerboat rudders usually consist of a brass or stainless steel blade mounted onto a steel spindle or stock, running in a tube. The tube is normally bushed at each end with sintered bronze bushes and the space in between can be filled with water-resistant grease. An added refinement on many commercial shafts, and one that can easily be added to home-made units, is the inclusion of a grease nipple to enable

The left-hand of these proprietary rudders is unbalanced and will require a relatively strong servo to actuate it. A balanced rudder (right) will take the load off the servo and reduce wear and maintenance requirements.

A typical three-point hydroplane stern assembly featuring unbalanced rudder and surface piercing propeller.

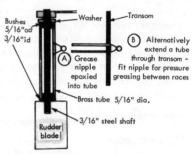

Bushes 5/16"od 3/16"id — Washer — Transom

(A) Grease nipple epoxied into tube

(B) Alternatively extend a tube through transom – fit nipple for pressure greasing between races

Brass tube 5/16" dia.

3/16" steel shaft

Rudder blade

grease to be pumped into the tube from a grease gun. A thin rubber washer, or better still an O ring, at the top of the tube and slightly nipped between the tiller arm and the top bush will give added protection against water ingress into the radio compartment. A Rolls Royce job is to bring a short copper tube soldered into the side of the rudder tube to a nipple fixed into the transom of the boat in order that greasing of the tube can be carried out from outside the model without the need to release the radio compartment hatch.

Many rudder tubes will have a thread at the bottom with a flange and nut to facilitate easy fitting into the hull. This is ideal for sports models and the smaller racing models, but ideally the area at the bottom of the tube should be reinforced, either with a hardwood block or application of glass reinforced plastic resin and mat, or a combination of both. If installing a smooth alloy or brass tube don't forget to roughen the surface with coarse glass-paper or a file to effect a suitable surface for the resin or epoxy to adhere to.

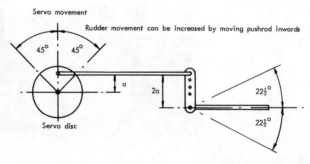

Servo movement

Rudder movement can be increased by moving pushrod inwards

45° 45°

a

2a

22½°

22½°

Servo disc

The amount of rudder movement required on any model is fairly specific and anything greater than 30 degrees either way is excessive. Above this value the rudder will act as a water brake, become less efficient, and particularly in a powerboat inflict heavy loads on the servo. In the worst cases the rudder can go 'over-centre' and lock, rendering total loss of control and a good chance of severely damaging the amplifier circuit in the servo.

As most servos give approximately 45 to 50 degrees of total movement, it is easily seen that the tiller arm needs to be about 1.5 to 2 times the length of the lever arm movement of the servo, giving some 25 degrees each way of rudder movement. If more or less rudder movement is required, then alternative hole positions can be drilled along the tiller arm for trial and error experimentation for the optimum set-up.

Vibration

Vibration has a much less dramatic effect on solid state radio equipment, that is radio with no moving or mechanical parts as per today's digital proportional systems, than it had on earlier systems which included valves and relays. The modern internal combustion racing engine turns over at around 15000 to 20000 revolutions per minute, that is over 300 miniature explosions per second. No wonder there were problems with equipment that contained mechanical or fragile parts.

This is not to say, though, that one can ignore protection for modern equipment against vibration. These high levels can cause an insidious slow breakdown of components and particularly soldered joints. The least that should be done is to surround the receiver and batteries with good quality foam and ensure that the servo mounting grommets are installed. All long runs of wiring should be supported, an easy task with plastic cable ties obtainable from high street electronic component outlets.

Aerials

Despite the fact that radio control will function satisfactorily at distances of up to 80 metres even if the receiver aerial is left inside the model, for any type of model powered by an internal combustion engine or a fast electric motor, it is essential that an exterior whip or telescopic aerial be mounted. Even if you operate alone, the extra signal strength obtained will markedly reduce the possible loss of control which is the

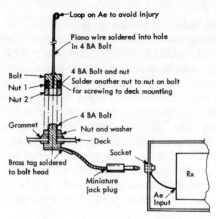

last thing one wants with a model propelled at not inconsiderable speed by a motor turning a propeller at high revs. A model out of control can be a dangerous object.

Whip or telescopic aerials can be purchased commercially or home-made. Telescopic aerials were in vogue a number of years ago and these can still be used on sports boats or launches. The disadvantage is that they are easily damaged and are relatively expensive. The whip aerial uses a piece of flexible piano wire and is almost indestructible.

The sketch shows one method of constructing a home-made aerial. The main essential is that a positive mechanical method be used to fix the aerial. Using just a banana plug and socket or similar electrical component is not recommended as the plug will eventually work loose, especially with engine vibration, and not only create electrical interference and bad contact causing loss of control, but can easily be dislodged at the slightest jolt – a not uncommon occurrence with multi-race boats.

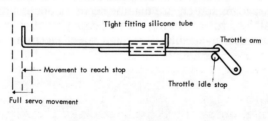

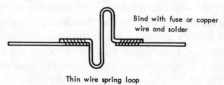

Don't forget to maintain the original length of the aerial wire as received with the equipment when purchased; i.e. if you intend to fit a vertical whip aerial of 16in length, the remaining wire between aerial base and receiver, assuming a 20in original wire, should be 4in.

Also, please ensure that a loop is bent on the top of the piano wire to prevent injury to eyes and person. Some modellers push a cork onto the exposed end. This is not really adequate as it can become dislodged. The loop is much safer.

The siting for the aerial should be as close to the receiver as possible and also as far away as possible from any potential source of interference or electrical noise, not always so easy, particularly with fast electrics, but aim for the best compromise.

Linkages and snakes

We have already covered this subject in some detail in the previous chapter, but there are a number of specific points to be considered with i.c. or fast electric models.

The pushrod system will be most satisfactory for the majority of applications, using the techniques described earlier. The ball and socket links came in for a certain amount of criticism when first launched some years ago as they were a trifle unreliable initially. However, they should now be accepted as the norm and can be used most successfully in powerboat models. Heavy duty versions are now available, but to find them you may have to investigate the accessory area in your model shop reserved for 1:8 scale i.c. racing cars.

Metal to metal clevises or links are acceptable with scale models but should be avoided with i.c. powered boats because of vibration. This is particularly likely to occur at the throttle linkage where engine vibration will generate vibratory rubbing at the pivot point, creating interference signals or electrical noise. Therefore a plastic end fitting should be used on the end of the metal wire or pushrod connecting to a metal throttle arm or tiller and vice-versa.

Commercial clevises usually have some form of keeper or self-locking device. Again this is particularly important with powerboats because of the vibration problem. A rubber band or a binding of soldered fuse wire works well on home-made systems.

For throttle linkages it is seldom possible to obtain a straight run from the receiver to the carburettor, usually because of the large fuel tank or because of the inconsiderate positioning of the throttle lever by many manufacturers. In fairness most engines are designed with model aircraft use in mind and the physical layout is obviously somewhat different.

If a metal fuel tank is used, one dodge, assuming you feel confident enough to handle a soldering iron, is to insert a copper or brass tube right through the tank to accept the pushrod. This is easier said than done, though, and fortunately the tube or snake solves the problem in a different manner. These consist of a stranded wire or nylon tube running in a larger but relatively close fitting nylon outer tube. The tube can be 'snaked' around obstacles. More space at the servo end is required to allow sufficient sideways movement of the inner core of the snake – unless linear servos are used – and it is important to fix the outer tube firmly to some part of the model structure at various points.

A wide number of clips for the latter task, and clevises and adjusters, can be used with snakes and investigation as to what is available at your local model shop would not be a waste of time. These components are inexpensive and it is not really worth all the bother of trying to construct your own.

The snake system is easy to use and has proved popular with model boaters, but it is this ease and versatility that causes modellers to demand too much from the system and expect it to run around the model until it resembles a miniature version of a complicated motorway interchange! Every bend creates more drag and end float, and poorly supported tubes can lead to centring problems, all of which puts a heavy load on the servo, drains the receiver batteries, and rather defeats the high resolution built into the servo. So, keep snakes as straight and as short as possible.

A straighter run to the engine can sometimes be obtained by running the snake along the side of the model and providing a bellcrank arrangement at the motor mount. This method also enables more adjustment to be obtained at the motor end, provides better clearances for the starting cord or belt, and as the arrangement reverses the mode of operation, it is useful if you do not have servo reversing and find the throttle operates in the opposite mode to that required caused by constraints created by the physical layout of your equipment.

As per the rudder linkage, a range of holes in the throttle lever arm or in the servo output arm will give flexibility in initially setting up the system so that full travel of the throttle arm matches full travel of the transmitter stick.

It is important that these movements do match. If, for example, the push-pull movement of the servo is greater than that permitted at the engine, then the servo will stall at one or other end of its travel. This state of affairs is very undesirable and will cause damage to the servo, either mechanically and/or electrically, and possibly even rapidly drain the receiver batteries to a point where control of the model is lost.

A slip link or spring loop can easily be built into the system to eliminate this problem. The simplest type of link is a piece of silicone

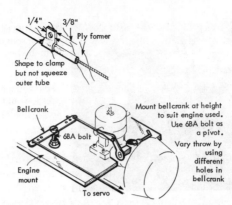

1/4" 3/8"

Ply former

Shape to clamp
but not squeeze
outer tube

Bellcrank

6BA bolt

Engine
mount

Mount bellcrank at height
to suit engine used.
Use 6BA bolt as
a pivot.

Vary throw by
using
different
holes in
bellcrank

To servo

tube slipped over the pushrod as shown. The spring loop is also fairly easy to make but requires a little soldering with fuse wire as binding.

With a modicum of care though, there is really no need for these devices which in effect condone a sloppy installation. It is a fairly simple matter to synchronise the movements so that full pushrod or snake travel equals full throttle arm travel by utilising different holes as mentioned earlier. What is important is that the idling speed is set up correctly, since in most cases the actual slow speed throttle position is determined by the idling screw stop adjustment. If the extreme movements of the servo are matched to this, then full throttle position will leave a little tolerance, and in most cases it will be found that a slight discrepancy at the top end will have no effect on maximum speed of the engine.

It is possible to make use of the trim control on the transmitter as follows. Back this off to the full throttle position and adjust the pushrod or snake so that when throttle closed is signalled by the transmitter the throttle moves to its normal idling position as established by the idling screw on the carburettor. The idling screw is then completely backed off, taking care not to go too far so that it drops out or can vibrate out. The transmitter will then give complete control with the trim in the forward (normal) position, but knock the trim back at tickover and the engine will stop, giving absolutely full control over the power plant.

Closed loop systems

In this system the servo pushes and pulls at the same time. This prevents the side and bending forces on a link and is a particularly efficient method of using all the power that can be generated by a servo without involving strain on the servo, so avoiding needless wear of the servo output arm shaft. The system is obligatory for radio controlled

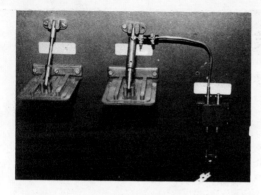

These trim tabs are mounted on the transom of the boat flush with the bottom and will affect the ride angle of the model. They are operated by a third servo and a hydraulic linkage which would be mounted inside the boat.

hydroplanes which operate with a completely unbalanced rudder. The method is shown in the previous chapter and can be assembled using pushrods, snakes or even multi-strand metal cable. Take care to keep everything free and smooth.

Extra functions

For the vast majority of power boat modellers, two-function radio will suffice. However, if you intend to take part in competitive multi and/or speed classes, a third or even fourth function might be desirable. Many engines offer the facility of mixture control or separate carburettors can be purchased which include this. As an engine gets hot its running characteristics will vary and it will usually require a slightly richer mixture. The mixture content may also vary slightly as the fuel tank empties, although most modellers use pressure fuel feed systems today. The latter is where pressure from the engine crankcase or the exhaust pipe is fed to the sealed fuel tank to give a constant pressure feed of fuel to the engine despite changes in fuel level. A third servo will be required to operate a mixture control lever.

Finally, the ride angle of a boat can be altered by trim tabs or plates mounted on the transom of the model. Most models will travel faster on calm water if their angle of attack is raised to reduce drag, but a boat set up to operate in these conditions will be decidedly unstable on rough water. Some trim tabs can now be adjusted by radio control either by a lever system or even by a hydraulic arrangement, but again an extra servo will be required.

Installations in model yachts

Most unenlightened members of the general public seeing a radio controlled model yacht in operation for the first time sooner or later come across and offer congratulatory noises on how the model performed, especially against the wind, and then spoil it all by some remark similar to 'Pity you have to have a motor in it though!'

So how does a yacht sail almost into the wind and what is required in the way of special equipment to facilitate effective radio control? Most readers will have some idea as to how an aeroplane flies. Air, a compressible fluid, is forced over the wing at speed either by a propeller pushing it or by the forward motion of the aircraft imparted by some other means of thrust such as a jet engine. If that air is persuaded to speed up by arranging for its flow to deviate around the top of the winged surface, a longer distance than the air flowing over the bottom surface has to take, the speeding up will cause that mass of air to reduce in pressure whilst over the wing. This reduction in pressure will exert a force on the wing which will try to move towards the lower pressure area – hence the wing lifts itself and the body to which it is attached, the plane, off the ground.

What has all this got to do with yachts? Well, the whole system can work in reverse, so to speak. That is, if an air flow moves around a static object stuck in its path, again it will try to lift it if it is the shape of a wing. But what if the wing is on its side and mounted vertically? Instead of lifting it will receive a sideways motion. Attach same to a hull and voila, we have a yacht. Obviously the wing or sail as it has now become will tend to try and move itself and the hull sideways, but as the medium in which the hull is working, water, is a much denser fluid than air and tries to prevent the boat moving in that direction, a compromise is reached and the boat moves forward.

Most people will know that an aircraft can stall and fall out of the sky. If the airspeed is not great enough, the airflow reaches a point where it tries to break away from the wing and eddies or spirals of turbulent air are formed. This results in loss of lift and gravity takes over. Aerodynamic engineers have come up with many ways to reduce this phenomenon, and one successful method is to fix a narrow additional wing in front of the main wing to produce a slot through which the air would flow. This slot reduces the speed problem and the air tends to stick to its working surface and continues to do its job.

The additional smaller wing becomes the jib on a yacht and the main wing is of course the mainsail. The slot is therefore a very important part of a model yacht and needs to be correctly set to obtain maximum performance from a given suit of sails. Most novices neglect this basic fact and are often amazed at the incredible improvement in performance which can be gained by simply getting the slot right. The effort produced from a correctly matched pair of sails will far outstrip the combined performance of the two sails considered individually.

It is also important that the sails maintain the correct angle of attack into the wind, so that while our yacht is going to carry on sailing quite happily when these conditions are set, the time will soon come when we need to go off in some other direction, irrespective of the wind setting. The only way we will be able to achieve this is to change the angle of the sails by rotating the mast, or more simply by altering the setting of a boom attached to the bottom of the sails. (Actually, there are now two classes which do rotate the mast.) This is the duty of the second function on a radio control yacht, rather akin to the speed control function on the power boat. There is one ideal setting for every direction in which the boat is sailing, and the whole challenge of sailing is to try and approach that ideal state of affairs under the infinitely variable conditions that wind and waves will throw at your model. It follows therefore that you will need to be able to adjust the sails through a whole range of settings.

In actual fact nearly 70 degrees movement requires to be controlled on either side of the centre-line. When the sails are pulled in towards the centre-line of the boat – commonly referred to as 'sheeted-in' – they will be approximately 10 degrees from the centre-line. Fully out will be some 80 degrees, that is nearly but not quite at right angles to the centre-line. The diagram shows the various sail settings required for different wind and boat directions.

Thinking back to our all-important slot, there is one saving grace. As long as the respective angles of the mainsail and the jib remain constant, the slot effect will carry on working satisfactorily. This therefore means that we only need one function to control both sails. Some experiments have been carried out where the jib and main are independently controlled, but unless the skipper is actually on board the craft and in a position to read every slight nuance of the wind's many changing moods, no apparent advantage can be obtained, and indeed there appears to be a definite disadvantage created by the complexity of such a system.

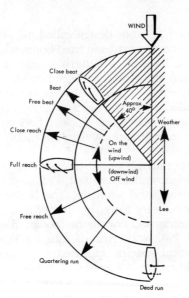

The force that our sheeting system will have to apply to pull in the sails against the wind strength will vary according to the sail area and the wind speed, but in very general terms at least 6-8lbs will be required for a large RA boat in a moderate to strong breeze. In most cases, around 3lbs will be adequate, but even this is far more than the largest conventional servo will be able to provide.

In recent years a number of special rigs have been designed with two basic thoughts in mind: one to simplify the rigging and derigging and secondly to reduce the forces necessary to control the sails to a point where a servo will be strong enough. This balanced rig, not dissimilar in theory to the balanced rudders discussed earlier in the powerboat

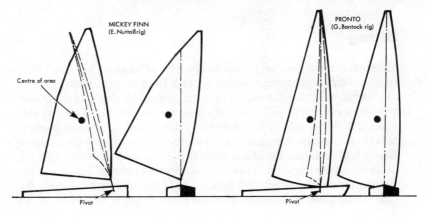

chapter, was first used in a one-design called the *Mickey Finn*. This utilises an ingenious cranked mast and fixed boom which has the effect of increasingly tilting the sail as it turns squarer to the hull. This effectively puts the sail into a more balanced condition the squarer it becomes. A standard servo can handle this rig in most conditions.

Another design called the *Pronto* has a straighter mast and balance is obtained by pivoting the mast some distance back from the sail tack. The rig does look more conventional than the *Mickey Finn* and seems to be more efficient.

In recent years experimental work has shown the importance of the relationship between downhaul, outhaul, kicking strap and backstay adjustments for varying wind strengths. The backstay adjustment is probably the least necessary to be capable of tuning during racing, whereas the kicking strap and flow in the foot are the most important variables. During the 1982 world championships in France, a number of complicated mechanical systems appeared to facilitate tuning of all these variables while racing. A number of simpler systems have now been devised and most operate by taking a sheet from an extra servo to a lever system which acts on the forward end of the jib boom or the aft end of the main, increasing the tension in the luff and reducing the flow in the foot of the sail at the same time. There are a number of variations on this theme which will be found in technical model yachting literature available from the Model Yachting Association, but it should be borne in mind when purchasing your radio equipment that if you perhaps intend to take up top competitive sailing, more than two-function systems may be required.

For all but the smallest models then, some special device other than a servo is required. This will either be a Sail Control Unit or a Winch. However, before we move on to these units in detail, we need to consider other basic installation requirements.

Siting

Although even in relatively small models the weight of 1.5 to 2lbs of the radio control equipment may not seem a large enough percentage of the overall weight of the model to worry overmuch about its siting, this weight nevertheless will have to come off the ballast of the model, making it fractionally less stable and competitive. As a consequence, radio boat draughts have tended to increase, in the classes where this is allowed, to maintain the status quo. It is important therefore that the radio weight be installed as low as possible in the model. The lower the weight, the more upright the boat sits and the more efficient are the sails. Unfortunately, throughout the earlier chapters of this book we

114

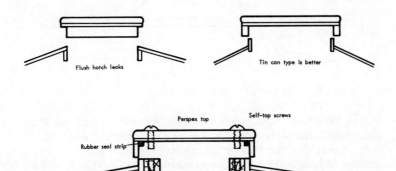

Flush hatch leaks

Tin can type is better

Perspex top

Self-tap screws

Rubber seal strip

Wooden blocks in blind corners

have pressed home that radio gear should be mounted as high and dry as possible.

As we have also said before, life is a compromise. If you want to be really competitive and are prepared to accept the risks, then sit your radio in a watertight box as low as you can; some modellers now even set their nickel cadmium batteries in resin in the actual bulb or keel of the boat!

But for the vast majority, the best place is just aft of the mast, near to the centre of gravity, and immediately under an access hatch. This hatch must be as watertight as you can make it, and much attention to detail must be undertaken to obtain this desirable state of affairs. Flush fitting hatches are prettier but much more difficult to seal than the raised variety. For the seals to be fully effective they need to be under slight compression when the hatch is closed. The most positive method is to use screw fixings. The sketches show methods utilising a conventional type of hatch. A popular approach today is to simply cover the hole with polythene sheet and seal the edges with a good quality adhesive tape such as freezer tape which maintains its stickiness in damp and cold conditions. Certainly not the most elegant or engineered of systems, but it seems to work for many.

The system discussed earlier for steam or i.c. powered models of screwing a transparent hatch down onto a flat coaming, sealed either with silicone grease or rubber, can be used. Unfortunately, it is not usually very convenient to section off the entire middle section of a yacht as can be easily done with the transom area of the powerboat. However, a large plastic box or wooden compartment can be made and either fitted directly under the hatch or its top can be made as a part of the deck for a more permanent installation.

For most though, the separate sealed box within the confines of the hull, but which can be removed for maintenance etc., will be the most favoured approach. The hole in the deck must be large enough for

115

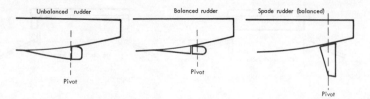

Unbalanced rudder   Balanced rudder   Spade rudder (balanced)

Pivot   Pivot   Pivot

access, yet sealed with methods described earlier. All the required equipment should be fitted in the box, including the winch or sail control unit. For the rudder linkage outlet, one can use the rubber bellows or balloon systems covered elsewhere in this book, and the on/off switch and crystal access can be similarly constructed.

If it is not convenient to position the switch in a location whereby it can be reached from a removable blanking plug, it may be possible to fit a wire arm through a hole drilled in the switch movement, and bring this up through a small hole in the hatch, suitably sealed with a greased rubber grommet. The switch will need to be mounted vertically. Bend the top of the arm into a loop and arrange the switch so that pushing the arm down switches the radio on.

Aerials

An underdeck installation is not recommended as yachts are nearly always sailed in groups and often at some distance from the operator. The wire can simply be led through a sealed outlet and led up a shroud, or the mast or the backstay. A neat move is to cut the wire short and connect it to the shroud plate, hence utilising the metal wire as the aerial. It will be necessary to insulate the shroud at a point which retains the original total length of the aerial. The insulator needs to be strong enough to take the tension on the shroud. If interference is obtained from the surrounding metal mast and other rigging, it may be beneficial to route the aerial to the stern of the yacht and use the backstay. Don't make the silly mistake, and it has been done, of fitting a whip aerial above the deck, forgetting of course to make allowance for the swing of the booms!

Rudders

If building from plans, the majority of which were drawn for free sailing boats, or perhaps converting an old free sailing model to radio control, it is more than likely that the rudder shown will be of the completely unbalanced type, front-hinged to a skeg or fitted to the trailing edge of a

A lever arm sail control servo. Note substantial mounting flanges moulded into the case. Compare with the drum winch on page 27.

keel. This will require excessive force from the servo and should be replaced with or modified to a balanced rudder as shown.

All modern radio designs will incorporate a spade rudder, and the most efficient form of this for a yacht will be considerably deeper than wider with the leading edge swept back to give a bottom chord or width about 50% of the top. The stock will be vertically through the mid-chord point of the top of the rudder. The final configuration should give approximately 40% of the area of the rudder ahead of the stock. Operation with this balanced design will be very sensitive and it will be found that much less than 30 degrees of rudder is all that will be required for the sharpest turns.

The rudder tube can be similar to that already described for powerboat models, but with the accent on keeping the weight down, so use aluminium alloys rather than steel. Bearings can be sintered bronze bushes or nylon. The tube may either come right up through the deck or finish below deck. The important fact is that in either case its top must be above the waterline of the boat, otherwise you will be inviting water intake. The only advantage with bringing the tube through the deck is easier supporting of the top of the tube. The disadvantage is another hole through the deck for the rudder linkage or servo output arm. All in all, the below deck arrangement possibly has the slight advantage.

Controlling the sails

Having covered all the other aspects of radio control in a yacht, we now come to the most important part of the system – the device which controls the sails via cords, known as sheets. A special type of servo is required to perform this sometimes arduous task. It can take the form of a winch or a giant servo with a large lever arm.

117

The latter arrangement has a greater following in the United States of America, mainly because of a successful design originally produced from a war surplus 'Drone' unit from the American Air Force. These units dried up a number of years ago but the company using them was foresighted enough to follow up with their own designed system. The arrangement is basically very simple and the principle may be employed by those who perhaps are keen to design their own. A small but powerful electrical motor drives a lever through some 120 degrees and the sheets are attached to the end of the lever. A similar system can be used on a standard servo in the smallest recognised sailing class, the 575, but even with the minimal 1sq. ft of sail area on this boat, quite often conditions are reached where the servo is not capable of pulling the sheets in against the wind and it is necessary to go about or gybe to turn, losing valuable distance.

For anything but the smallest models it really is a waste of time trying to make a servo perform sail control. Any mechanical system devised can only be made to give the desired amount of movement at the sail by lever or geared systems which will always by the laws of physics be less powerful than the original force output by the servo, and be drastically

Below left, this Nylet 10-rater Pacemaker installation shows sheet emerging from deck at rear and passing through fairleads to boom and jib attachment hooks. Right, all lines above deck and a substantial screw-on access lid to the radio compartment on this unusually shaped R36r.

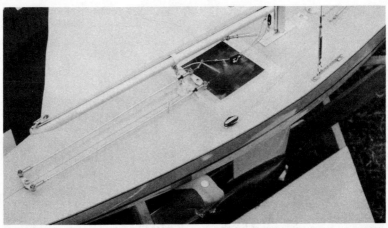

This installation shows a taped down hatch cover and an above deck closed loop rudder linkage.

slow to boot. And speed is important in any model which is to be used for racing, no more than 3 to 4 seonds from fully out to fully in.

If speed isn't important, for instance in a scale sailing model, the ancient but useful screwed-lead system may be worth a second glance. This system was originally employed as a means of rudder control in early radio control systems. A long screwed rod is rotated by an electric motor in either direction as determined by the function selected from the transmitter, and a threaded jockey or travelling nut, prevented from rotating by a guide, moves along it. The sheets are attached to the jockey and led away through suitably positioned pulleys. For a 10in movement, the time taken will be approximately 10 seconds, depending of course on the motor speed and the gear ratio employed. The disadvantage with the system is that it is not proportional. The motor will be started by microswitches which themselves need to be operated by a servo. The sheet will only move when the transmitter stick is keyed in one direction or other, and the servo will be employed simply as an expensive microswitch operator.

The device which is now almost universal in its application is the drum winch. This consists of a servo amplifier with a high reduction gear ratio driving an output spindle which is fitted with a single or sometimes twin-drum. Whereas a servo only provides about one third of a complete revolution, the drum can rapidly spin through several revolutions allowing the sheets wound around the drum or drums to be let out or pulled in by as much as 20ins. A worm gear will be incorporated somewhere in the gear train, and by virtue of its method of operation, the worm gear prevents a positive torque from travelling

119

The Futaba drum winch described in detail in this chapter.

back through the system from the sail force, which would otherwise have to be counteracted by the winch amplifier and create a constant current drain on the batteries.

The latest units even include an electronic method for adjusting the total sheet travel from say 20ins to 15in by altering a small trimmer hidden behind a waterproof seal in the winch casing.

A typical specification, in fact a Futaba winch, is as follows; twin drum approximately 1in in diameter giving a winching speed of 3.9in/sec (100mm/sec) with a torque of 111.2oz. in (8kg. cm) at 6 volt. The amplifier section of the unit is taken from the receiver via the normal receiver plug; the output motor takes its supply from a separate 4.8 or 6 volt battery. The overall dimensions, excluding the drum, are 1.5×2.1×3in (37×53×76mm) and the weight is 8.8oz (250gm).

There is a drum cover which includes four leadouts for the sheets and the whole case features suitable mounting holes which enable the winch to be set on its bottom or its back. Both the lead-out wires are sealed with a waterproof compound.

As can be quickly seen from the above specification, this is an entirely different animal when compared to a servo. The much larger motor would quickly overload and flatten a normal 500 milliamp receiver pack, and it is normal for a separate battery supply to be provided for powering the winch, which will have a separate wiring harness to suit. The voltage required is nominally 6 volts and with a capacity of 1.2 ampere/hours.

Practically all the units available for purchase in the UK will work with almost all of the various makes of radio gear without modification, however it is sensible to make sure that your intended purchase will function satisfactorily with your set of radio control equipment. You may have to supply your own plug if your gear is an old or unusual model, although most winch manufacturers will prewire for you at the factory when ordered, sometimes on receipt of a slight extra charge.

Most modern winches are well waterproofed by the manufacturer, but additional protection can be provided by wrapping in waterproof tape or coating the unit with a latex adhesive such as that supplied for carpet binding.

It is also important that the winch be securely mounted wherever it is situated. The tension on the sheets can be quite substantial and peak loads from gusts can be unbelievably large.

Sheeting systems

Most model sailing yachts operate with a synchronous sheeting system, that is the main and the jib are controlled by the one winch drum or drums, or the lever arm of a sail control unit. The usual material for the sheets is sea fishing line or braided Dacron, a remarkably strong and flexible cord, yet with minimal stretching and low friction. The sheets will obviously need to pass through the deck at some point on their way to the booms. This is a potential point of water ingress and whilst this cannot be entirely prevented, it can be markedly reduced by careful design of the leads. Typical designs are shown in the photos. Low friction materials such as PTFE or more commonly available Nylon are best, while metal or rubber bushings or grommets are completely unsuitable.

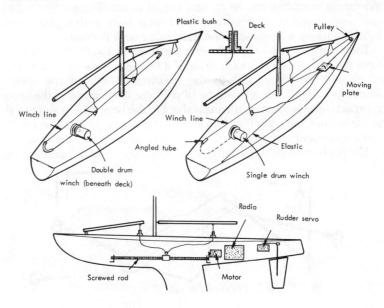

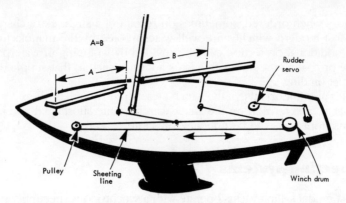

The leads can be angled away from the direction of flow should the boat ship water, which will restrict water intake. Alternatively, a tube can be brought some distance above the deck and the sheets led away through wire tripods above the tubes, giving an even greater protection.

If you opt for the system whereby the winch or SCU is mounted just below the deck with the output spindle protruding through a suitable hole, the latter can be sealed by a greased rubber O ring.

A winch or SCU will give true proportional control over the sail movement. In other words, assuming the sails are sheeted right in and the transmitter stick is at the topmost point of its travel, by lowering the stick to its mid point, the winch will rotate its drum by 50% of the total movement available; the lever arm would move through 50% of its maximum travel. Both systems would then hold at that point until another change was made to the transmitter stick position.

The simplest method of arranging the sheets is to take both directly from the drum, or from each drum if a twin-drum winch. Sheet total travel will then be equal to the maximum travel of the winch. Sometimes the two drums will be of different diameters and the usual approach here is to attach the main sheet to the larger drum and the jib to the smaller, allowing the main sheet to be attached further aft on the main boom and giving a better mechanical advantage to the system.

The problem with this arrangement is that the wind pressure on the

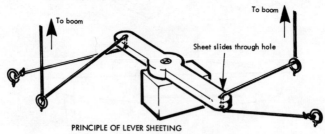

PRINCIPLE OF LEVER SHEETING

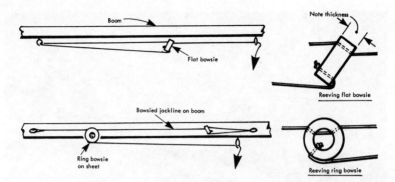

sails is the only force keeping the sheets taut. In calm conditions or a sudden lull, the sheets can go very slack and unwind from the drum. Artificial tension can be imparted on the system from a length of rubber as shown in the figure. The disadvantage here is the extra load applied to the winch, which of course has to extend the rubber. This can be minimised by using a lengthy piece of rubber, but then one starts running into installation difficulties.

A much better arrangement, and one now used almost universally, is for the winch drum to drive an endless line along the hull, either inside or outside depending on the winch location. The drum is sited aft and the line taken forward, around a pulley and back aft to the other side of the drum. The sheets can then be attached to this line and both will move identical distances. As long as they are then attached to the booms the same distance from the boom pivot points, identical angles of boom swing will be generated. The obvious disadvantage with this system is that the winch must be sited at one end or other of the model to avoid fouling the sheet take off points on the drum.

If you have a twin-drum winch, it can be positioned wherever you require to suit your radio box installation. The system required is shown in the figure. The sheets can be attached at any convenient point, making sure that both sails are drawn in or let out together. This incurs

Extended servo arm provides lever action on this *Mickey Finn*. Sheet lead is a wire tripod and rudder pushrod is also sited above deck.

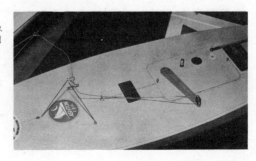

123

French modellers go in for jib twitchers, flow control and other secondary controls, as well as ultra-light spars. These can be advantageous in the light winds in which they normally sail.

attaching them either both ahead or aft of the sheet leads on the deck.

However careful you are in measuring and determining the amount of sheet required for main and jib, it will be a very difficult task to ensure that when everything is secured, the two sails lie at the correct angles. There is obviously a need for some sort of extra trimming or fine tuning device. This is achieved using a small fitting called a bowsie. These can be either flat or ring type. The former can be cut from 2mm thick plastic and the holes should only be slightly larger than the cord diameter. The correct way to thread them is to feed the cord through one end hole, through the required eye and then through the other hole of the bowsie from the same side as the first hole was threaded. Ring bowsies are cut from sections of thick walled plastic tube and should have three holes not quite at 120 degrees. Thread as shown.

An above deck sheeting and rudder installation. Note the crystal switcher on the hatch.

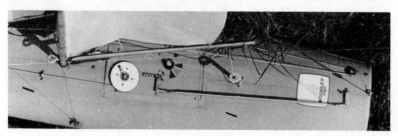

Another above deck installation, this time using a lever arm system. Note the drawer handle for lifting and transporting the model.

If you join the sheet just below the boom with a hook and eye, it will be an easy task to disconnect and derig the mast and sails for transport.

The lever unit sheeting arrangement, assuming a double lever which the majority are today, is best set up between the sheet leads so that the lever ends are moving with the same relative motion to each lead, otherwise it will be necessary to take one of the sheets past the unit and reverse its direction. The system shown will double the travel of the sheet and will be necessary for all but the smallest yachts.

In general

Take care with the whole installation, double check everything for smooth operation as you proceed, and don't rush it. Because there isn't an engine to complicate matters, many beginners run away with the idea that installation in a model yacht is a doddle. It isn't, unless you want a disaster on your hands. But take things steadily, produce a good workmanlike craft, and you won't be the unfortunate individual who spends more time with his model in pieces while everyone else is enjoying the blow.

9 Specialities

Much of the first part of this chapter will discuss the task which seems to cause the most difficulty amongst radio control model boaters – that of controlling the speed of an electric motor and hence the model in either a scale or fast electric environment.

For many years there were no proprietary speed controllers available and it was left to the modeller's ingenuity to devise a suitable system. Most resorted to a simple switching circuit built around microswitches or Government surplus units. The microswitch is now readily available and with a little care, quite effective circuits can be utilised.

The very simplest is shown in fig 9.1 which just provides an on/off facility at full speed in one direction only. By adding a second microswitch and a suitable resistor, full, and an intermediate speed, determined by the value of the resistor, are obtained, fig 9.2.

Many variations on these themes can be worked; two switches and two batteries can be set up to give full speed forward and half speed astern, fig 9.3, or with one battery forward and astern – again a resistor can lower the reverse speed, fig 9.4.

Microswitches can be obtained from the High Street electronics shop and will need to be fitted adjacent to the servo output disc. The disc must be shaped into a cam so that as it turns it operates the microswitch or switches as required and according to the position of the transmitter stick. It is fairly straightforward to make up a ply shelf with a cut-out for the servo body and sufficient space to accommodate the microswitches alongside. Most microswitch cases are moulded with small mounting holes drilled through them and they should be mounted with nuts and bolts. Servo tape is not good enough. Initial setting up is a trifle fiddly and may take some time; however, it is important that the cams do not bind against the switch cases or even the switch button to prevent servo damage.

A number of manufacturers produce plastic moulded switch trays that fit over and around the servo. Some come complete with ready shaped cams and ultra-small microswitches.

As a guide to the size of resistance required, a nominal value of 10 to 15 ohms will suit most scale boat and small launch motors. It is

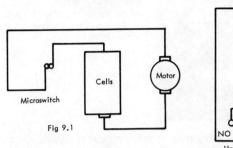

Fig 9.1

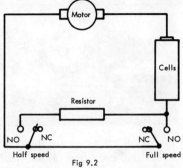

Fig 9.2

important though that the wattage rating – a figure which determines the amount of power that the resistance can dissipate without getting too hot and eventually failing – should be at least equal to the wattage rating of the motor.

Many books also give circuits for potentiometer controllers. A potentiometer is an electrical device which alters the resistance of a circuit by sliding a conductive wiper across and around coils of continuous wire, themselves wound in a circular form. These devices were once easy to obtain in that they were the only way of controlling the resistance in a 'power' circuit. That duty though has now been taken over by thyristors, heavy duty transistors, and the power potentiometer has almost disappeared. Potentiometers are still very much used in

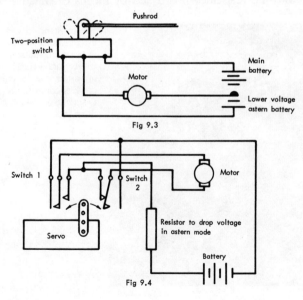

Fig 9.3

Fig 9.4

127

A simple cam driven microswitch device which fits on the top of most servos for speed control.

electronic circuitry, but these units have nowhere near enough power to control even one of our small motors.

If you don't feel inclined to dabble with microswitches and bits of resistance wire – by the way an old electric fire element from the local Council Tip makes ideal resistances, but you won't be able to solder to it and will have to use mechanical connections such as crocodile clips – there is fortunately an easy way out that is not too expensive, yet is reasonably successful and used by many modellers. The unit in question is known as a 'Resistance Board' or sometimes just a 'Wiper Board'.

The two names give clues as to how these devices operate. An insulated thin board has a special resistive foil material fixed to its surface in various shapes and areas over which a wiper arm attached to the servo output arm can be moved. The wiper will make electrical contact with the resistance board and by means of suitable circuitry,

The resistance board seen in this ultra-small tug model will fit in practically all scale models and is quite effective. It is important that the correct capacity controller is purchased to suit the current loading of the drive motor.

Three electronic speed controller which all replace a servo and work directly from the receiver. Left and middle are both designed for boats and include reverse mode; that at right is a car controller and there is no reverse mode, but it will handle higher powers, hence is more suitable for fast electric models.

control is achieved in relatively small increments of motor speed. The fineness of control will depend on the number of tracks on the board; the normal supply is three to five changes in forward and astern. This will be quite adequate with the majority of scale model requirements. Some of the boards are mounted separately from the servo and are operated by a short pushrod, but later models actually fit on top of the servo and the wiper arm bolts straight onto the top of the output disc.

Resistance boards need to be chosen to suit the power of the motor and are available in a variety of sizes; for instance 2, 3, 5, 8 and 15 amps. If in doubt as to the size required for your application, err on the higher side.

So if these units are so marvellous, why spend considerably more on an electronic controller? Well, there are limitations. They rely on the rubbing contact of the wiper on the board and will only operate reliably as long as both surfaces are clean and dry. And there lies the rub; boats are not dry! However, if your maintenance is regular, they can give very good service. If they become corroded or, as is more likely, oxidised, don't try to clean them with glasspaper or emery cloth. This quickly ruins both surfaces. A hard pencil rubber and perhaps a little switch cleaner will work wonders.

The second limitation is one that applies to all types of resistance controller. They cannot be used for reversing wound field motors without additional switching being incorporated. These types of motors are now seldom used for models, though.

Electronic speed controllers

Decidedly the best method of controlling an electric motor from modern proportional radio control equipment is the fully electronic speed controller which takes the place of a servo and plugs directly into the receiver. A typical unit would be about twice the size of a receiver and in addition to the wire going to the receiver, there will be four larger heavy duty wires, two for the battery supply and the other two for connecting to the motor.

There has been much development in these units over recent years, mainly due to the explosion in interest in radio control cars and off-road buggies. These vehicles have a voracious appetite for reliable high power, units, and this development has resulted in a wide range of units now available for all purposes.

Most controllers will be capable of providing full proportional control from full speed down to stop and usually a reduced speed performance in the reverse mode. These parameters can be trimmed to suit the radio equipment in use by small electronic trimming screws on the controller. This task is not difficult and full instructions will be included with your choice. Reversing is going to be required for scale boat use, but will not be wanted for a fast electric. Many of the top of the range car units do not include reverse mode, so check before buying.

In earlier units it was necessary to include a full-speed relay for installations where maximum performance was required, as the circuitry in the controller used a very small amount of power. This was not to be a problem with scale boat and sports use, but the fast electric fraternity require every watt of power to go into the motor and not be absorbed by the speed controller device, however small. Today's units, however, use devices called MOSFETS, which are almost 100% efficient, and the relay is no longer required, so reducing dramatically the weight and size of the controller.

The electronic controller does not work by reducing the voltage as do the resistance methods, but alters the amount of time that current is fed to the motor. The breaks in supply happen extremely rapidly and the motor is fooled into continuous running. The beauty of the device is full speed and power at one extreme, with the ability to turn the motor, under load, so slowly that the propeller revs can be counted at the other!

Car controllers also nearly always include a controlled electrical feed to the receiver. It is a not very well known fact that the battery feed to a receiver can be through any of the servo sockets and not just the socket reserved for the battery plug. In most instances this will have no positive use as obviously plugging the battery feed into a servo socket prohibits the use of that socket for its intended purpose. However, if the device being controlled can generate the correct voltage for the receiver to work on this can be fed back down the line to the receiver. This is the principle used by many car controllers. The advantage is that the model does not have to carry an extra battery supply for the receiver and this

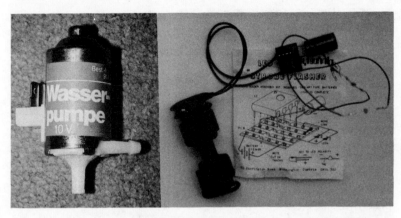

Two of a wide range of accessories which can be bought, a water pump unit for operating fire monitors and a strobe flasher suitable for police and similar boats.

can be important in a model where space and weight are important factors. Hence such a supply will be of use to fast electric modellers.

Beware, though, for if the main drive battery source drops below the required receiver voltage, as it undoubtedly will in the case of a fast electric model using a heavy current drain, the receiver will cease to function and radio control of the model will be lost – not a dire situation with a model car where you can walk out and retrieve your errant model, but a trifle awkward with a boat!

As we stated earlier the speed controller is controlled directly by the receiver responding to the transmitter signal and the connecting wires carry very small currents. However, the output circuit of the controller

This complete drive and rudder unit simply needs a large hole in the transom of a model. A Kort nozzle can be added if desired.

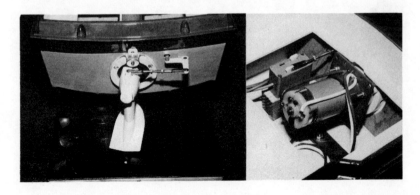

An example of a bow thruster unit. The propeller unit can be removed for maintenance.

has to handle the high ratings required by the motor. These currents can peak at very high levels and it is usual to incorporate a heat sink to dissipate the heat produced by the unit. This is normally a thick piece of aluminium plate and the controller should be physically fixed to the plate by bolts, etc.

Electronic speed controllers are very reliable as long as they are chosen correctly in the first place and are not mechanically or electrically abused. The higher the current rating required, that is the higher motor power to be controlled, the more expensive the controller will be. If you only intend to operate scale models, it is a waste of money to buy a high power output controller, but if your present or future requirements lean towards fast electrics, a high output device will be required. The heavy duty model can be used completely satrisfactorily on lighter duties but the opposite most definitely does not apply.

Controllers are normally rated in maximum continuous amps and volts. For instance, a 12 volt 10 amp job will handle 12×10 (Volts $\times$ Amps) = 120 watts.

A Voith Schneider drive unit which fits into the bottom of a hull with five vertical blades protruding down. The whole wheel rotates and by varying the angle of attack of the blades, propulsion can be in any direction. Right, this steerable propulsion unit can be rotated through 270 degrees.

Make absolutely certain that all connections have been correctly made before switching on or plugging in the battery supply to the controller. Many controllers are electronically protected against incorrect cabling up and no damage will be caused if inadvertently connected incorrectly. But not all are protected in this way and incorrect connection of the battery supply will almost always blow some of the electronics, requiring the complete unit to be returned to the manufacturer. And furthermore most manufacturers fit a tell-tale device in the equipment which will tell them if the controller has been connected incorrectly – and in most instances the guarantee will not cover this improper use.

If you are useful with a soldering iron and electronic components, there are one or two companies offering kits for speed controllers. The saving will be in the region of 25% of the cost of a proprietary unit, and unless you are really confident, then stick with the latter. They will certainly be smaller than a home-made unit, and trouble-shooting if the home-built doesn't work first time can require sophisticated equipment to locate the fault.

Other services

It is a sad fact that most modellers only use their radio control equipment to operate the rudder and speed control systems on their model. The potential of radio control for operating other services is very neglected, particularly in the UK, it seems. Most, if not all, of our regattas are for boats to be steered around a course, whereas many events on the Continent are for individual and group model displays. The NAVIGA World Championships include categories for individuals and teams of modellers to present ten minute displays for public consumption. These range from complete sea battles with guns blazing, sirens wailing, ships sinking and being ultimately recovered by salvage vessels, through to trawl and drift fishing operations with casting and recovery of the nets.

At club and private levels, modellers can still include working gun turrets, fire monitors, winches, cranes, signalling lamps, sirens, launching and recovering of small daughter craft, lowering and raising anchors, etc. There are all sorts of possibilities limited only by the time and money the modeller is prepared to spend. Many of these devices can be built with much ingenuity and little expense, but all will require some method of control.

Full-house radio equipment designed primarily for model aircraft use will offer six functions and require six servos, leaving four for auxiliaries once the rudder and speed controls are taken care of. It is

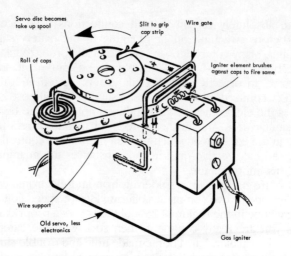

Servo disc becomes take up spool

Roll of caps

Slit to grip cap strip

Wire gate

Igniter element brushes aganst caps to fire same

Wire support

Old servo, less electronics

Gas igniter

not very often, however, that all the special functions will be in operation at one and the same time, and therefore one or perhaps two servos could be made to operate some form of sequence switcher.

A device similar to that shown in the figure could operate five switched services, three controlled by movement of the transmitter stick and hence servo one way and the other two with the opposite mode. Typical services switched could be Radar on, Warning lights on, Siren on in one direction of the servo; position Fire Monitor and Pump Water in the other. A ratchet operated transmitter stick will be the best for this type of operation, as this will maintain the servo in its chosen operation until the next service is selected. The limitation is that only one service at any one time can be operated and it will be necessary to move quickly through an unwanted service to select one at the end of the switcher.

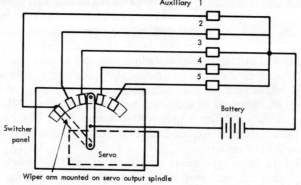

Auxiliary 1
2
3
4
5

Battery

Switcher panel

Servo

Wiper arm mounted on servo output spindle

Sequence Switcher

This German fireboat has working monitors, crane, radar, lights, sirens, anchors and lays a carpet of foam! Radio (right) switches 12 units plus normal functions.

There are a number of Continental radio control equipment manufacturers who produce gear particularly for the boat modeller who specialised in display work, and between 12 and 32 extra services can be switched through a special receiver and control box. Unfortunately this equipment is not available in this country at present and it is also somewhat expensive, but is may be worthwhile keeping one's eyes peeled if on a Continental holiday. A number of domestic suppliers manufacture a 'black box' which can give up to six extra services from one function. This unit plugs into the receiver in place of a servo and acts as an electronic version of the mechanical switching device mentioned previously.

Devices such as sirens and ships' whistles will obviously need to be operated from the radio gear, however it is worth mentioning at this point that other forms of electronic noise generators are now becoming available designed around proprietary sound generator integrated chips. A number are available commercially, ranging from ships' diesels to a tug's steam engine. They are wired into the drive motor supply leads and start operating as power is fed to the motor. If an electronic speed controller is used, some of these devices will pick up the changing pulses from the speed controller and use them to speed up or slow down the simulated engine noise in synchronisation with the speed of the motor and hence model. Radio Control Boat Modeller magazine has published circuits for many of these devices and a browse through back issues at the local library might be worthwhile.

Radio control is such a wonderful medium and opens up so many possibilities for realistic simulations of full size vessels of all types. Try not to waste your investment.

10 The power pack

The universal standard for radio control equipment power, both transmitter and receiver, is the dry pencell or its equivalent in rechargeable nickel cadmium format, the different characteristics of which we will discuss later.

Early radio control systems utilised valve circuits and required high voltages – 120 volts for transmitters and 45 volts for receivers – and the dry batteries were substantial in size and expense. Fortunately the low voltage devices, transistors, integrated circuits, etc., that are now universally used in modern equipment only require low voltages which can be supplied by the type of cells mentioned above.

Although there has been a coming together of the prices of dry cells and nicads, as nickel cadmium cells are now known, the former are still relatively expensive. They are used (principally to reduce initial cost) in almost all one or two function sets at the economy end of the market, but for the higher current drains required by three to six function outfits, nicads are generally fitted.

Dry cells

For many years the PP range of batteries, 9 volt, as used in domestic radio receivers, were mainly used, especially in transmitters, which need between 8 and 10 volts depending on design, with pencells reserved for receivers. Recent years, however, have shown a trend towards pencells for transmitters as well. The size (U7) is available world wide, as are ready-made plastic battery boxes to accommodate 2, 3, 4 or 8 cells. This one international physical size incorporates three basic types of dry cells, all of approximately 1.5 nominal voltage: standard, high power, and endurance (alkaline-manganese). At first glance there appears to be little to choose between standard and high power except that the latter (HP7) type are more expensive. A little testing, however, will show that the voltage supplied by the HP cell is higher than that supplied by the standard; the voltage falls at a slower rate with the HP cell and it has a higher capacity. An additional benefit is that it is of leakproof construction, i.e., the corrosion-making electrolyte will not leak out and cause damage if accidentally left standing in the equipment for long periods when exhausted. The extra initial cost of HP7 type cells is therefore worthwhile in view of the extra running time and the advantages detailed above.

The alkaline-manganese type of dry cell can be used and is also of 1.5 volts nominal, with a much bigger capacity and slower rate of drop off than even the HP cell. It would obviously be a much better choice, giving at least five times more life, but again, it has to be discarded before it is fully exhausted and therein lies the difficulty – choosing that throw-away moment. Obviously a transmitter which has a neon voltage-sensitive light which flashes intermittently when the voltage falls to an unsafe level, or better still a battery voltage or radio frequency meter which gives a reasonable indication as to battery condition, are useful items.

The receiver indication is not so straightforward. Ideally one would recommend replacing receiver batteries before every outing, but at over £1 for four, this obviously becomes very expensive. Perhaps one answer would be to avail oneself of a reasonably accurate voltmeter, one that can measure to tenths of a volt. Most electronic component suppliers advertising in electronic hobby magazines offer panel meters for around £4 to £5, a sum that could be quite quickly repaid if you can extract 10 to 15% more life from your cells. To determine their condition, switch the equipment on and after a minute or so read the voltage and discard cells reading 1.1 volts or lower. Also it is false economy to replace individual cells in a pack – the new one will be rapidly 'dragged down' to the level of the others. Always change a complete pack.

The variable world of battery supply. Top and right, a lead-acid gel cell, foreground dry pencells. The remainder are nickel cadmium cells of different capacities.

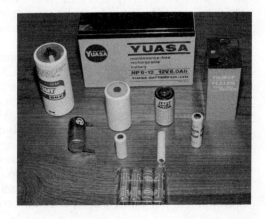

Left, the first nicad cell was the German DEAC, still available, though cylindrical nicads have taken over. DEACs cannot be fast charged. Right, a mains charger capable of giving a large number of varying output rates at anything up to 36 volts.

Nicads or deacs

These are rechargeable cells based on nickel cadmium and have a nominal voltage of 1.2 volts and are known as secondary cells, whereas dry cells are called primary cells. The latter is an arrangement whereby it is only possible to transform chemical energy into electrical energy, and the cell can only be revitalised by the renewal of the active chemical constituents, something not possible outside of the battery factory. If the chemical reaction is of the reversible kind, electrical energy being converted into and being stored as chemical energy when the cell is charged, and chemical action being transformed back into electrical energy when the cell is discharged, the cell is known as an accumulator.

With a nominal voltage of only 1.2 volts, at first sight one is prompted to ask how they can replace 1.5 volt dry cells. The answer is simply current delivery – nicad discharge voltage is substantially constant regardless of load, and what is more important, remains constant until the battery is almost completely exhausted. As a result a much more reliable energy source is therefore supplied to the equipment and intermittent high current drains (such as a stalled servo) do not drop the voltage to danger levels. The cells are completely sealed, are more compact as no battery box is required with button cells (see later), and no maintenance apart from keeping them dry is necessary. Weight is about the same as the equivalent energy source in dry cells. The only disadvantage is initial cost, some three to four times that of dry cells, plus of course a charging device, between £9 and £25, depending on sophistication. So, taking these prices into consideration, a recharge-

138

able power source plus charger will be paid for after some ten to twelve battery changes in dry cell. The frequency of operation will decide whether or not it is worth changing to nicads.

Initially, rechargeable cells were only available as the button type, manufactured by a German firm called DEAC, hence the name has stuck, like Hoover. These cells are manufactured in a wide range of capacities. However, the sizes of most use to us are 225, 500 and to a lesser extent 100 and 1000. The numbers refer to their capacities, a 225 is 0.225 ampere hour and a 500 is 0.5 ampere hour capacity. These two sizes cover the needs of most transmitters and receivers, although the 1000 size is ideal for high output duties such as sail winches. Button cells can be welded together in any number and provide equivalent battery voltages as follows:

Cells	2	3	4	5	6	7	8
Voltage	2.4	3.6	4.8	6.0	7.2	8.4	9.6

Most modern radio control equipment uses dry cells in the pencell configuration and nicads are now available in these international size cases. The rechargeable equivalent to the pencell is of 0.45 ampere hour capacity, again at 1.2 volts. Some of these cells may be described as vented and suitable for fast charging. These are perfectly suitable for dry cell replacement.

When installing battery packs, as mentioned in the chapters covering installation, provide adequate foam packing to prevent vibration damage, which in extreme cases can fracture wires, and movement during a crash – the relatively heavy weight can cause considerable damage if allowed to bang around a radio box or compartment. It is also worth checking wires for corrosion at regular intervals.

Left, a typical modern charger which can handle a variety of cell pack sizes and which automatically switches off when the cells are fully charged. Right, a fast charger which will charge for a period set by the operator on the time switch. Both units use a 12 volt car battery as the primary source.

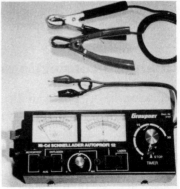

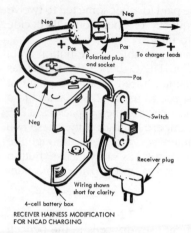

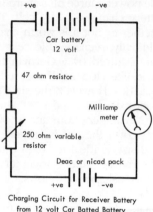

RECEIVER HARNESS MODIFICATION
FOR NICAD CHARGING

Charging Circuit for Receiver Battery
from 12 volt Car Batted Battery

As we stated earlier, most receivers operate on a 6 volt supply and by simply changing the dry cells for nicads, you will be reducing the voltage from 6 to 4.8 volts. For the vast majority of receivers this will not cause any problem and they will continue to operate quite satisfactorily on 4.8 volts. Indeed many receivers actually reduce the 6 volts to just over 4 volts for their own internal use. Also, the nicads hold their voltage right through to the end of their life whereas dry cells start dropping in voltage from the moment they are made. You should check first, though, when buying a dry cell outfit that it will operate on a lower voltage at a later date. The transmitter will be similarly affected but from many years' experience where a straight replacement of nicads for drys has been carried out, no problems have been found. Some equipment comes with a blanking connector which takes the shape of a pencell and is inserted in the battery pack if dry cells are used, but is replaced with a nicad if upgrading. This method retains the same or a very similar battery voltage for both systems.

Charging connections

Replacing the dry cells with the nicads is the easy bit. The next stage, if you are going to make a proper job of it, is to fix a charging connection to the receiver and the transmitter. You can of course continue removing the nicads for recharging as if they were dry cells being replaced, but you will need connections and cases to hold the nicads while they are charging, so why not let the existing battery box and transmitter case do that duty?

140

This British-made charger will cope with a variety of charge requirements, using a timer and operating from mains electricity.

The receiver is relatively straightforward. Most receivers will have been supplied with a battery harness, a length of wire which usually has a plug to insert into the receiver at one end and is connected to a plastic battery case at the other. Also it is normal for a switch to be included. The simplest method is to solder two lengths of wire, preferably red to the positive and black to the negative, to the terminals of the battery case. Make sure that all surfaces are clean by using a small file or wet and dry paper (used dry) and that the soldering iron is hot. Use at least a 25 watt iron. Apply solder to the wire end and quickly to the case terminals. If the terminals do not 'tin' immediately, remove the iron and make a better job of the cleaning. If the iron is left in contact with the metal terminal stud for more than a few seconds, you will have a battery case minus terminal as the plastic melts at quite low temperatures. If both wire and terminal are tinned, then apply heat again to the wire and apply both iron and wire to the terminal as speedily as possible. Repeat with the other terminal. The other ends of your two leads should be soldered or connected to a suitable polarised socket – not a plug as there is then a danger of a short if they become inadvertently bridged by a scrap of metal or wire. The output leads from your charger should be connected to the plug part of this connector, making absolutely certain that you have the polarity correct, i.e., the positive or red goes to red and the negative or black goes to black. The switch in the original harness will prevent the charging supply finding its way back to the receiver.

A similar principle is applied to the transmitter, but in this case you will not normally have two terminals that can be reached from the outside of the case. It will be necessary to take the back off the transmitter and then a number of different approaches are possible.

141

The important point is not to connect the charging point after the main power switch, always before. In many cases you will be able to solder direct to the terminals outputting from the battery compartment. Again take great care and be quick as the plastic cases melt at low temperatures. If you cannot get to the battery compartment terminals it may be possible to tap off the battery side terminals of the switch. Follow the red and black wires from the battery compartment terminals and solder to the first convenient point. The other two ends of your leads can then be attached to a socket as for the receiver. Obviously it would be a good idea to use the same type of socket for both the receiver and the transmitter, but this will depend on availability and a suitable fixing point on the transmitter.

With care one can usually feed the wires back through the battery compartment and if small enough sockets are purchased there may well be room for these to sit inside the compartment.

Alternatively one can obtain miniature jack-sockets and plugs from High Street stores such as Tandy, and the socket can be mounted by carefully drilling a suitably sized hole in the transmitter case. This is much the professional method, but you should take a long, hard, look at where you intend to mount the socket. Is there enough room internally for the socket and its wires? Is there any likelihood of the rear of the socket shorting or touching other electronics? Finally, of course, if your equipment is still within warranty, then any dismantling or modifications to the internals will invalidate your guarantee.

Capacity

Many modellers are confused by the terminology associated with battery capcity and perhaps a paragraph or two on this subject will be of benefit. C or capacity stands for the total amount of energy which can be obtained from the battery, when fully charged. The nominated capacity, for example 0.5 ampere hour, is that which will be obtained when the battery is discharged at such a rate or current as will bring it to a fully discharged state in ten hours, hence C/10 or the ten hour rate. Another way of expressing 0.5 ampere hour is 0.5×1000 or 500 milliamp hour. Theoretically, it would be possible to take 500 milliamps from the battery for 1 hour, or 5 milliamp for $500/5 = 100$ hours, or any combination of current and time which when multiplied together produces 500 milliamp hour. This statement must be treated with some caution, though, as the majority of batteries perform best at or near their specified hourly rates, i.e. C/10 in our example. This characteristic is much more important when using fast charging techniques, but for electronic use practically the full nominated capacity is available.

Charging

As stated earlier, equipment supplied with rechargeable cells initially comes with a charging unit for plugging into the mains supply, and all that is necessary is to follow the instructions carefully. Chargers can be purchased separately, with or without a meter for checking the charging rate. The type which includes a variable control and a meter can be very useful and it is worth paying the extra for the increased versatility that such a unit will give. The correct recharging rate at the ten hour rate, which is the generally accepted norm, is easily calculated in the following manner.

Divide the ampere hour capacity of the cell by 10. Taking our previous example of an 0.5 ampere hour cell, we obtain 0.5 × 1000/10ma = 50ma. This is the required charging current. Theoretically then, obviously at a ten hour rate, the latter is the charging time. However, some energy is lost during charging and it is necessary to provide for this loss; a figure of 1.4 times the length of time is normal – hence charge of 0.5 ampere hour cell at 50 milliamps for 14 hours. Batteries are rarely fully discharged after use and are usually recharged before the end-point is reached, obviously to avoid equipment failure. It is thus difficult to decide how much charge a partially discharged battery will need. Fortunately, at the ten hour rate, no damage will occur to the battery even if it receives a 100% overcharge. However, constant overcharging will result in a shorter life. If an accurate voltmeter is available, we would recommend discharging fully to 1.1 volts per cell before recharging.

This is the basis of the recycling devices now available and if you do not possess such a unit, here is one method of checking your battery capacities. Apply a load to the batteries using say a 20 ohm resistor. This will apply a 1C load and for the test batteries should be fully charged. Measure the time it takes for the batteries to drop to a voltage of 1.1 volts per cell, i.e., a 4.8 volt receiver pack has four cells, hence measurement of time ceases at 4.4 volts. The average current through the resistor will be 500 milliamps, hence:

With 225 packs, using the 20 ohm resistor will give a 250 ma load.

It is a useful facility to be able to charge nicads from a 12 volt car battery. The car battery and pack to be charged should be connected in series. Suppose the battery pack is 4.8 volts and the car battery 12 volts, then the voltage across the resistor will be 12 – 4.8 = 7.2 volts. If the pack is a 500 and we require a charge rate of 50 ma, then we must perform a simple calculation based on a physical law named after the person who discovered it, Ohm. It states that in any circuit where current is flowing the voltage V will equal the current I (amps) times the resistance R (ohms). So, applying the formula:

V = IR or R = I/V, R = 7.2 v/0.05 a = 144 ohms, 150 ohms being the nearest obtainable. A wattage rating of 1 watt would be suitable.

By incorporating a variable resistance of say 250 ohms and a milliamp meter, one would be able to vary and check the charge rate. The 47 ohm resistor is included to protect the nicad pack if the variable resistance was inadvertently set to zero.

How much sailing

The answer to this question depends upon the size of the battery pack in terms of capacity, the number of servos in the model, and what type of model.

For most power boats, multi-racing, steering, or speed, a 500 pack should provide power for at least two hours – assuming that linkages and servo operated controls are free. A binding control will take very large currents and reduce operating time dramatically. Most scale models, with their lighter loaded control surfaces, should last slightly longer, but the addition of horns, lights, and operating ancillaries will obviously have a marked effect. However, if one wishes to save weight, very important in fast electrics, a 100 milliamp hour pack will last something like 15 to 20 minutes. At the other extreme, yacht sails controlled by a sail winch take a relatively large drain and the fact that most yacht races are longer than those for power boats means it is worthwhile considering a 1000 milliampere hour pack.

Storage

Dry cells have a relatively short shelf life and should not be bought in large quantities and stored. It also pays to purchase cells from a dealer with a high turnover for maximum freshness.

Nicads can be stored charged or flat, and simply cycled a few times when bringing them back into use. Choose a cool, dry spot. Remember that if stored in a charged state, don't expect them to be ready for use immediately on withdrawal from storage as they lose 5% of their charge per week.

Suppression

All motors and any electrical devices which incorporate movement will create sparks during their operation, and electric motors are par-

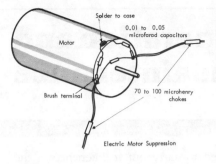

Solder to case

0.01 to 0.05 microfarad capacitors

Motor

Brush terminal

70 to 100 microhenry chokes

Electric Motor Suppression

The dangerous result of incorrect fast charging nicads. The owner was very lucky to ecape with his life and suffered severe lacerations and bruising. (Photo Ray Bridgen).

ticularly prone to this phenomenon. These electrical disturbances can generate wide-band signals which under certain circumstances can cause interference to radio reception. Many motors are suppressed with suitable electronic components to minimise this problem, and radio control equipment includes circuits and protection against this sort of interference. Nevertheless, if your installation does suffer from inexplicable interference problems, it may well be worthwhile adding some extra protection to the drive motor or motors.

Some model shops will be able to sell you a package of components and instructions as to how to fit these to your motors, but if you are not fortunate enough to have such a thoughtful supplier in your locale, you will be able to purchase the necessary bits and pieces at the High Street electronics store or through mail order to one of the many electronic houses.

For maximum protection you should connect, by soldering, a single capacitor of .01 to .05 microfarads between the brushes, plus a 70 to 100 microhenry choke in each lead.

Servos and winches will already be protected by the manufacturer.

11 Operation and maintenance

There should never be any need to carry out maintenance at the lakeside. It will, of course, already have been carried out at home! So, before venturing forth, let's take a look at maintenance and fault finding.

Maintenance

Start with the power source, the battery. Inspect it for physical damage or leakage if a dry cell, although of course it will have been replaced long before such an occurrence can take place, but this is a reminder to remove dry cells at the end of a sailing session if it is going to be some time before the next outing. Nicads need to be inspected for bulging cases, a tell-tale sign that they have been abused by rapid overcharging. It is not good practice to charge nicads being used for radio equipment rapidly – except in emergency. Also inspect for corrosion around the terminals or soldered connections, especially the negative lead. An electro-chemical reaction causes this lead to deteriorate before the positive, and a feature of the corrosion is that it applies to the whole length of the wire, not just at the point where it is soldered to the battery. If you come across this problem, it will be necessary to replace the whole length of wire.

You can carry out a voltage test, but unless the equipment is switched on, this will be meaningless. Switch on for at least 30 seconds before making a measurement.

Bad or loose wiring is a common reason for equipment failure, and starting from the battery, check all connections for broken strands and make sure that none of the wires foul any of the servo mechanisms or their output shafts. See too that wires are not pulled tight, but have a little slack, so as to prevent vibration fracturing them. All wires should be supported close to their soldered connections, which also helps prevent vibration fractures.

How long has the on-off switch been fitted, and have there been any recent occasions where it needed a couple of on/offs to make it work? If so, discard it and replace. Try the High Street electronic shop if your local model supplier can't help.

Check the receiver for loose plugs and crystal socket. If in doubt, replace or find someone competent to do it for you if you don't feel qualified yourself.

Again, with servos, check for broken leads and replace if confident – otherwise seek expert help. Check for excess wear at the output arm. Some manufacturers will supply mechanical parts separately for maintenance. If twitchy operation is obtained and this is not due to interference, it may be caused by dirty feedback potentiometers in either the servo or transmitter. These can be cleaned with spray switch cleaners such as Electrolube. Don't use the WD40 type lubricants on electrical components as it leaves a sticky waxy deposit behind which will attract dirt and dust.

Relays, wiper type speed control boards, etc., should have their contacts cleaned with one of the proprietary switch cleaners as mentioned above, or special rubber cleaners sold in electrical accessory shops. They should not be attacked with emery cloth or glasspaper. If they have reached this stage of degradation then they need replacing.

Before venturing forth, make sure that all supposed watertight joints are watertight and that everything is finally in place, plugs and sockets fully home and secure, etc., and charged, of course. Also, a quick check to make sure that you didn't leave the transmitter or receiver switched on after the last sailing session – and don't forget to switch them off after the checking procedure. You won't be the first to arrive at the lakeside with flat batteries.

Other points

Moving away from the more specific and detailed checks required for radio equipment, there are a number of other actions that should be taken before submitting to the overwhelming urge to dash off to the nearest water to try your new model before the paint has dried.

You have made a suitable stand, haven't you? We know it's a bind of a job, but it is absolutely essential. Some very forward-thinking manufacturers are even including the timber in their kits, and for power boaters there are a number of ready-made stands-cum-toolboxes in glass reinforced plastic. You can even get them the same colour to match your power boat hull. You will not be able to start the model properly if an i.c. boat; sooner or later the rudder or propeller on a scale boat or fast electric model will be damaged, while the yacht will be impossible to rig.

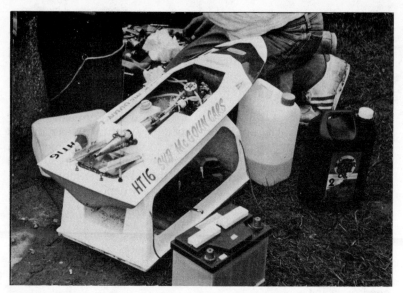

A multi-racer needs a substantial stand and this grp unit has the added advantage of raising the model to a more convenient height for maintenance and starting. Car battery powers electric starter.

Make sure that all hatches fit properly, that propeller shafts are free, properly aligned and lubricated, that the propeller is properly secured, that engine bolts and exhaust systems are secure, that there are no leaks or splits in fuel and water cooling tubes, that fuel tanks are clean and secured, that the rudders and masts are vertical, that all rigging hooks and eyes on a yacht are secure, there is freedom of movement of booms, and the sheets are not going to snag.

Phew! What else do we need? Well, whatever type of model you are going to run, you will need a toolbox and some spares. Obviously the power boat modeller is going to need a much more comprehensive set of tools and spares than the scale man or the yachtsman. Essential items are fuel, starting cord or starter motor (and don't forget to fit the drive belt before installing the motor), starter battery, glow-plug battery, clips and spare glow-plugs, propellers, spanners to fit flywheel and propeller shaft nuts, and some means of retrieving an out-of-control model such as a ball on the end of a fishing rod line, spare crystals and pennants, screwdrivers, elastic bands, hand cleaner, oil, dry cells, cleaning rag and/or paper kitchen towels, and in addition, for the fast electric enthusiast, adhesive freezer tape for fast electric hatch battening, spare cells, charger and leads, battery and voltmeter. And don't forget a tube of quick-set epoxy and some instant cyanoacrylate adhesive.

Yacht stands need to be even higher to clear the fin and are seen in wood or metal tube or quite often, as in this French example, converted from a sturdy camp stool.

One of the beauties of model yachting is that you can certainly avoid having to carry around the workshop that seems necessary with powered models. The usual problem with a yacht is that you don't forget a vital spare but you may forget a vital part of the model. As the rigging and fitting out is nearly always carried out at the lakeside, it is quite easy to forget a mast or a suit of sails or a keel. A compartmentalised box is probably a good idea to put all the bits and

Tools can be kept safe yet handy in one of the many plastic cases now available, and if filled with foam, indentations can be specially shaped, highlighting lost or borrowed items.

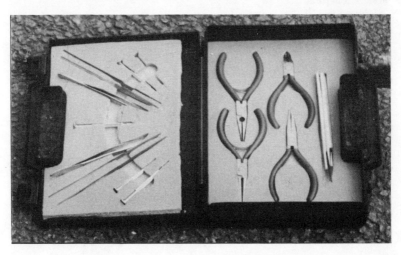

pieces in. If the areas are labelled you can soon see if something vital has been forgotten. A screwdriver and some pliers, together with some spare piano wire and rigging wire should be carried, plus some sheeting cord, insulation tape and again a tube of epoxy and instant glue will be useful.

And finally, depending on your lakeside local circumstances, you might need Wellington boots, or more likely with a yacht which may need to be taken out some distance to find water deep enough to accept the keel, a pair of fisherman's waders.

At the lakeside

Before switching on, ask around and make sure that no-one else is on your chosen frequency, or if a peg-board system is in operation then take the corresponding peg and attach it to your transmitter aerial. If it is the first time of operation then a quick radio range check would be advisable and will instil some confidence. Reduce your transmitter aerial to about a quarter of its normal operating length and walk away from the model while waggling the rudder. If you retain control up to about 10 to 15 yards distance, all is well. By the way, there is a golden rule with regard to switching on and off radio gear. Always switch the transmitter on first, followed by the receiver, and when sailing is finished, switch the receiver off first. This will prevent your receiver

Scale boat stands can enhance the display of a model, as does this one. An old fruit box can subconsciously do the opposite and implant the idea that perhaps the model is also a bit suspect in parts.

from being affected by other transmitters which may be close enough to cause your receiver to find a spurious signal and perhaps cause damage to your servos.

If an i.c. powered model, start the engine and make sure that the vibration of the engine is not causing radio glitching. This will not occur if the receiver has been packed in a foam bed as recommended.

Finally, when the big moment arrives, release the model and spend a little time assimilating the feel of the controls before running fast if a power model. If you have never used radio control before the greatest problem will be initial orientation, especially when the model is coming towards you. Don't worry, it is a bit like riding a bicycle, but a faster learning curve and less painful, fortunately. The answer is always to think and react as if you were aboard the boat and not as a land-based observer.

After sails

At the finish of a session, don't neglect cleaning the model and transmitter, especially removing oil and fuel with a proprietary cleaner or good old washing-up liquid. Allow everything to dry thoroughly before putting away or closing the hatches or compartments, etc. Dry out the silica gel bags, if fitted.

Cleanliness and ensuring a thorough drying out at this stage will take

Boat stand in grp; plastic crate to carry starting equipment and a closed tool, spares and radio box shows a professional approach. If a starter battery is needed and the car cannot be parked nearby, a trolley helps!

Starting an internal combustion engine powered model is much easier with a stand and a friend to hold the glow plug clip in place. The forward flywheel on this engine means that the starter band can be removed easily.

a few minutes and save many hours at a later date. Prevention is better than cure!

Problem solving

If the worst does happen and all systems are no-go despite all your preparation, then don't despair. Modern radio control equipment is very reliable and component failure is extremely rare, unless the gear has been ill-treated. Loss of control is seldom caused by equipment failure or by interference from an outside source. It is much more likely to be the effect of one or more of the following:–

    Weak or discharged batteries
    Dirty or poor connections
    Stiff or sloppy linkages
    Water ingress

A suspected failing battery can be checked by a voltmeter with the cells connected and the unit switched on as suggested earlier. Replace with freshly charged nicads or new dry cells.

If you have a suspected faulty servo, the best way to check this is to exchange the plugs at the receiver. This will immediately identify whether it is the servo at fault or the receiver. Substitution of a friend's receiver or transmitter will identify problems in that area, but don't forget to change crystals to match your transmitter. Crystals have been known to stop working, especially if subjected to vibration, so try another pair. It is not too difficult to accidentally bend the legs of a crystal when inserting it into its socket. Bending it back with a pair of pliers is then quite likely to permanently damage it. So take care as they are not cheap items.

Check wires for continuity by means of a voltmeter or 1.5 volt battery and a torch bulb. Sometimes wiggling of the wire will highlight a broken wire hidden by insulation, a common cause of intermittent operation. Check the on/off switch in particular and clean contacts with switch cleaner or, better still, replace it.

Intermittent operation, particularly at some distance from the operator, can be caused by a poor or broken aerial wire. Follow it right back to the receiver, again checking for breaks within the insulation.

If still no joy and other, perhaps more experienced, modellers cannot help, the only recourse is to send it back to the manufacturer's recommended repairers, making sure that it is adequately packed.

Unusual launching frame, more of which are being used as models become heavier and bulkier, like this North Sea anchor handling vessel. (Photo David Metcalf).

Don't go fiddling around inside the receiver or transmitter as attempted repairs by non-specialists can create more problems and perhaps result in permanent and expensive damage.

Drying out

If the worst does happen and everything gets a bath, the first thing to do is to disconnect the batteries. It is the electrolyte effect of electricity and water combined that does the worst damage. Most of the solid state components used in the radio gear will not be affected by a short dunking in fresh water, but salt water is a different ball game. The best action in the latter case is to take the gear to the nearest fresh water source and attempt to wash out all traces of salt water. Then, and only then should you dry out the equipment with the car heater, or hair dryer or fan heater, or anything that features a moving stream of warm, dry air. Servos can be dried out by carefully removing the case screws and withdrawing the bottom part of the case which surrounds the amplifier. Be careful when removing the top part of the case as this usually supports the gear reduction shafts, so remember or make notes of how they are assembled. Dry out as above, but don't attempt to take the motor or feedback potentiometer apart. The motors are sealed at the factory and disturbing the potentiometer will upset the centring and trim of the system. If the motor contains moisture it is unlikely that even forced ventilation will remove it and it will have to be returned to the manufacturer for dismantling and drying out.

Appendix 1
Clubs and Courses

The advantages of becoming a member of a model boat club, to the beginner who intends to take a serious interest in his chosen hobby, cannot be too strongly emphasised. Not only will will he see what is being done by others, but he will find the more experienced members only too ready and willing to assist him to make progress in whatever line of boating he may choose to take up; there is also the stimulating effect of the various competitions which are part of every club's activities. All these advantages are denied to the home worker, and thus many enthusiasts find it worth their while to join a club, even though it may be some considerable distance from their locality.

Beginners are sometimes deterred from coming out into the open with their first efforts by the fear that they will meet with a critical attitude on the part of the experts who are to be found in practically every club. We can, however, state quite definitely that such fears are nearly always groundless and that a sympathetic outlook towards the other man's efforts is part of the personality of the majority of modellers, and this is especially so in organised clubs.

Most model boat clubs in Great Britain are comparatively small, comprising usually around twenty members. In the past, clubs tended to specialise in certain aspects of our hobby, only natural, as obviously an uncommitted new member will tend to be drawn into the ways of an already established group. However, various sections are now springing up within clubs. For instance, a typical club could have a straight-running, a radio control power and a scale section. Indeed, some recently formed clubs cater for power, scale and sail modellers – a trend which we hope will continue as only good can come from appreciating the other person's point of view.

The two major associations in the United Kingdom are the Model Power Boat Association (GB) Ltd., formed in 1924, and the Model Yachting Association dating from 1911. They control the competitive activities of the clubs, with particular emphasis on national competitions, look after the interests of model boaters with local and national government bodies, and provide insurance cover within their

Club life is great. The anticipation of a fast electric race at the water of the Cygnets club, Maidstone, Kent.

membership fees. The MYA can be joined as an individual but the MPBA only as a member of an affiliated club. The whereabouts of your nearest club can be obtained by sending a stamped addressed envelope to the respective secretaries:–

Model Power Boat Association
General Secretary
c/o Model Boats
Argus House
Boundary Way
Hemel Hempstead
Herts HP2 7ST

Model Yachting Association
Russell Potts
8 Sherard Road
London
SE9 6EP

Courses used in competitions

Most events in Great Britain for power boat models, other than scale, are run on the NAVIGA world model powerboating organisation's courses. For radio boats they can be broken down into speed, steering, and multi-boat racing.

The speed course is a shown in fig 12.1 and consists of an equilateral triangle of 30 metre sides. The object is to navigate the course as shown in the fastest possible time. Current world record for 15cc powered boats is round 12.9 seconds. A good club time would be about 19 seconds. This course is used for radio speed competitions in the UK at club and National level.

The NAVIGA steering course is shown in fig 12.2 and is also based on a 30 metre triangle. It is designed to test the skill of the pilot in manoeuvring his model, a specific functional model built for this class and not a scale subject, through a pattern of obstacles, with the prime purpose of passing between each gate without touching any of the buoys and completing the course in the fastest time. Each gate has a set width as shown and carries specific penalties if touched or missed. This

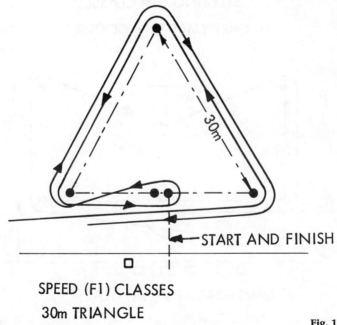

START AND FINISH

SPEED (F1) CLASSES
30m TRIANGLE

Fig. 12.1

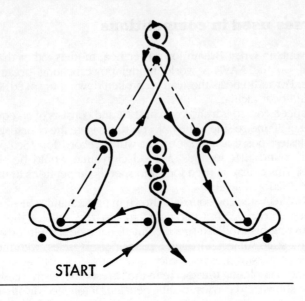

START

STEERING (F3) CLASSES
CHRISTMAS TREE COURSE

Fig. 12.2

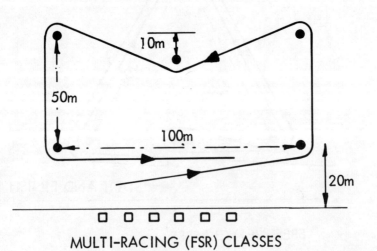

10m

50m

100m

20m

MULTI-RACING (FSR) CLASSES
'm' COURSE

Fig. 12.3

course is used for steering events throughout the UK although there is little support for the class today. A good club time is 45 seconds; the world record is just under 30 seconds.

There are official sizes laid down from NAVIGA for multi-racing and these sizes are adhered to if the water is large enough to accommodate it, see fig 12.3. A slightly smaller course is used for fast electric models. Clubs use the same or similar course for their events, but many UK clubs circulate the course in a clockwise direction as opposed to the NAVIGA recommendation of anti-clockwise. We always have to be different, after all! There is usually a Le Mans type start where all boats leave the pits at the given signal. A maximum of twelve boats can take part in any one race. There are many variations of length of race, from 30 minutes to 2 hours, and there have even been some 24 hour races. In some events the boat which records the maximum number of laps in a set time is the winner whilst other races are for a set number of laps, similar to the Grand Prix car racing system. Multi-racing is the most popular powerboat classification.

There are a number of special speed courses used for straight line speed and circuit record attempts. These are primarily based on American courses and are slowly gaining some following in the UK, and latterly in NAVIGA. Similar to full-size record attempts, the boat must

Again at Maidstone, but this time a scale event brings admiring interest from public as well as fellow club members. (Photo Ray Brigden).

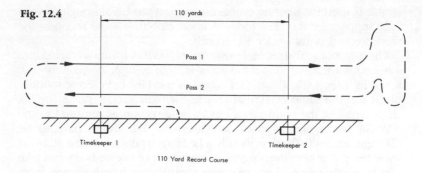

Fig. 12.4

110 yards

Pass 1

Pass 2

Timekeeper 1   Timekeeper 2

110 Yard Record Course

complete two runs on the course, one in either direction, without returning to the bank. The course is shown in fig 12.4 and this is one of the few classifications in model boating which gives the competitor and driver a true record of his model's speed. Current UK speed for the most powerful i.c. class is 60mph. The Americans, who have practised this form of model boating as one of their major classifications for many years, now have one or two boats which have recorded over 100mph.

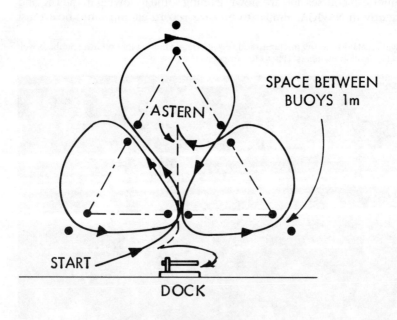

SPACE BETWEEN
BUOYS 1m

ASTERN

START

DOCK

SCALE (F2) CLASSES
CLOVERLEAF COURSE

Fig. 12.5

There is a recommended course for scale boats from NAVIGA, see fig 12.5, but for some reason this is not very popular in Great Britain and has not even been used for the National Scale competitions. Most British events involve steering around a course consisting of conventional pairs of buoys, but including scenic hazards such as wrecks, lighthouses, oil rigs, etc. The result is more attractive to the spectator, but often confusing to the competitor who has to learn a different course at every meeting. All courses for radio scale models tend to have

Most British scale regattas require a docking manoeuvre and negotiations of buoys representing their full-size cousins. Two tugs (above and below) make their way around a course at the Maidstone club's annual scale event. (Photos Ray Brigden).

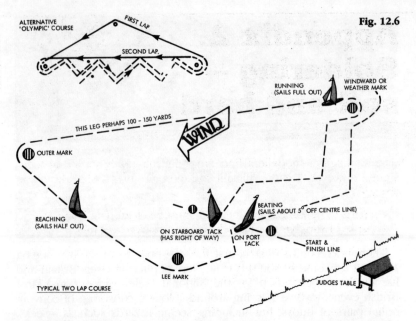

Fig. 12.6

an astern manoeuvre and a docking test, where the model must be steered astern through a pair of buoys without striking them – only a minimal number of attempts are allowed – and the model must be brought to a halt within an allotted space and remain stationary for three seconds without manipulation of the transmitter controls; both very difficult tasks.

The course for model yachts is normally based on a triangle which is set out by the Officer of the Day to give beating, running, and reaching legs as far as is possible. The number of laps of the course to be covered in any one heat depends upon the length of the course and the strength of the wind, but in general heats are expected to last approximately 8 to 10 minutes. Up to twelve yachts will compete in any one heat and points will be awarded for the order of finishing. A schedule will have been drawn up before the start of the first race and as far as is possible, yachts will race against different competitors in each heat.

Each class model yacht must be certified and measured to make sure that it conforms to the class rules, by registered measurers who will be found in most model yacht clubs, before it will be allowed to compete in competitions.

162

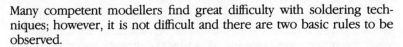

Appendix 2
Soldering –
soft and hard

Many competent modellers find great difficulty with soldering techniques; however, it is not difficult and there are two basic rules to be observed.

All parts to be joined, and the iron, must be clean. The iron must be capable of supplying enough heat for a quick, clean job.

For soft soldering, that is joining of solderable metals such as copper, brass, tin, etc., resin-cored solder as sold in electrical component and most car accessory shops is to be preferred, as the flux which prevents oxidation of the surfaces during the soldering process is included as a resin within the centre of the solder itself. This is quicker and cleaner than using separate tins of greasy flux. Also, a small, electric iron is better than one of the older irons that need to be heated in a flame. They are usually much too big and awkward for the finesse required in most soldering jobs on a model. Look for a size of 25 to 40 watts. The former will easily cope with most jobs, but it may refuse to solder wires to the larger nicads and the 40 watt size will be required.

Switch on the iron to enable it to come up to its correct working heat. Most electric irons are temperature controlled and will maintain the correct working temperature. Bare the wire ends if making a connection, or clean up components that are to be soldered together by the application of fine wet and dry paper, used dry. Do this immediately before the soldering operation. Leaving the cleaned surfaces for no more than a few minutes will allow oxidation of the surface to begin and it is impossible to make solder adhere to an oxidized surface. Touch the end of the solder to the wire or the component, and bring both into contact with the tip of the hot and cleaned iron. Cleaning of the iron can be accomplished by a quick wipe, when hot, with a dry rag or piece of paper, but don't get burnt. The solder will melt and run over the wire or component. Immediately remove the iron and allow to cool. Now repeat the procedure with the other piece of wire or component to be joined. This is called tinning. Now simply bring the two wire ends or the components together and apply heat from the iron. The solder should quickly melt and run together. Remove the iron and hold the joint steady for a few moments to allow it to cool. The solder should have a glossy, hard surface. If not, clean everything and start again.

Soft solder is very acceptable for electrical connections, but for high strength and heat resistance, silver soldering, sometimes known as hard soldering, will be required. The melting point of soft solder is between 200 to 400 degrees Centigrade and this will melt if used on the exhaust system of a model internal combustion engine, for instance. Propeller blades and small components, but which need to be physically strong, plus engine installation supports and exhaust systems, and model yacht rigging fittings will require silver soldering.

The solder is an alloy of copper, zinc, cadmium and of course, silver – which is why it is rather expensive – however, a little goes a long way. It melts at temperatures between 600 and 900 degrees Centigrade, so an electric soldering iron will be of no use. Also, a much greater area of the object that is to be soldered will need heating to prevent overcooling of the point being soldered by conduction.

A small burner will be required and whilst the older paraffin types can be used, there is an ever growing range of gas fired units now available, some with an oxygen cylinder attachment which can bring temperatures up to levels allowing welding of small components. A special flux is required for silver soldering, but which performs exactly the same task as its soft solder counterpart, preventing oxidation.

Ensure that the surfaces to be joined are clean and mate nicely together. They will have to be physically restrained from being blown apart by the flame if small or if they cannot be clamped in suitable supports. This can be achieved by binding them together with fine iron wire, trying not to let the wire come into contact with the surfaces to be joined. The flux will most likely have been purchased in powder form and will need mixing with a little clean water to a smooth paste that does not run. Form a hearth on the bench with some firebricks to conserve the heat source. Make sure they are fire bricks: you may be able to rescue some from an old fire-grate. Don't use ordinary bricks as these will shatter or even explode under the high temperature flame. Smear the joint with the paste; light and adjust the burner flame until a clear blue cone can be seen. Heat the workpiece overall to bring up its working temperature to reduce heat loss from the joint, and apply the tip of the cone to the joint. Bring up to red heat and apply the solder stick carefully. Its end should instantly melt and flow all around the joint. The paste will have turned into a clear, glassy liquid just prior to this heat point being reached. You may be able to position small pieces of silver solder around the joint before heating it, but the danger with this method is that you may not initially include enough solder and will be left with gaps which are then difficult to fill.

The workpiece can then be left to cool off or it can be quenched in water. Quenching will make copper alloys softer, but steel is made brittle and may become too brittle. In this case, heat the workpiece again until the oxide layer is blue to red and quench again. This process will soften, toughen or temper the steel. The reason for quenching is that the flux will break off due to the sudden contraction, otherwise you will have to remove this rather stubborn layer with a wire brush or emery paper. A file will not touch it as it is too hard.

Appendix 3
Useful facts and figures

Length	1 inch	= 2.54 centimetres
	1 foot	= 30.479 centimetres
	1 yard	= 0.9144 metre
	1 centimetre	= 0.393 inch
	1 metre	= 3.28 feet
Area	1sq. in	= 6.45sq. centimetres
	1sq. ft	= 9.29sq. decimetres
	1sq. yd	= 0.836sq. metre
	1sq. metre	= 10.763sq. ft
Volume	1cu. in	= 16.387cu. centimetres
	1cu. ft	= 0.028cu. metre
	1 gallon	= 4.545 litres
	1 litre	= 1.76 pints
	1cu. cm	= 0.061cu. in
	1cu. metre	= 35.314cu.ft
Weight	1 pound	= 0.453 kilogramme
	1 kilogramme	= 2.205lb
Imperial to metric:	Inches × 2.54	= centimetres
	Yards × 0.9144	= metres
	Gallons × 4.546	= litres
	Pounds × 0.4536	= kilogrammes

Miscellaneous: One gallon of water weighs 10lbs, contains 277cu. ins, or 4.54 litres.

One litre of water contains 61cu. ins, weighs 2.2lbs, or 1 kilogramme.
One knot = 1 nautical mile per hour.
One nautical mile = 1.1528 statute miles.
One cu. ft of water weighs 62.42lbs and contains 6.24 gallons.
One pound of water contains 27.7cu. ins or 1/10 of a gallon.

Appendix 4
Wire sizes

Stranded insulated wire should be used for all circuit wiring and this is normally specified according to the number of strands and the diameter of each strand in inches. For example, a 7/006 would consist of seven strands of .006in diameter wire. This is a recommended size for normal circuit wiring. For drive motor supply leads, etc., heavier wiring such as 40/0076 would be required.

Insulated wire is available in a wide range of colours and some form of colour coding should be used to facilitate ease of checking when problems arise.

Appendix 5
Microswitch
circuits

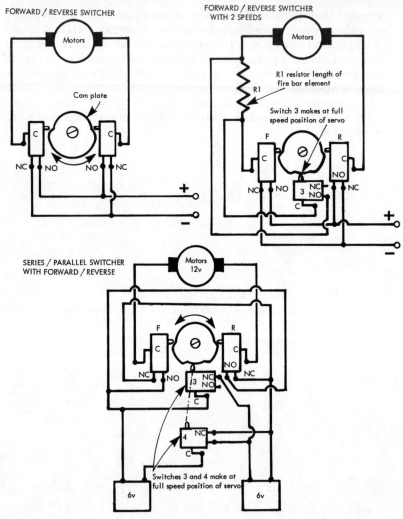

FORWARD / REVERSE SWITCHER

Motors

Cam plate

C   C

NC ● ● NO   NO ● ● NC

+
−

FORWARD / REVERSE SWITCHER
WITH 2 SPEEDS

Motors

R1 resistor length of
fire bar element

R1

Switch 3 makes at full
speed position of servo

F   R

C   C
                NO

NC ● ● NO   3 NC   NC
                   NO
              C

+
−

SERIES / PARALLEL SWITCHER
WITH FORWARD / REVERSE

Motors
12v

F   R

C   NO

NC ● ● NO   3 NC   NC
              3 NO
              C

4 NC
   C

Switches 3 and 4 make at
full speed position of servo

6v   6v

Appendix 6
Manufacturers

Great Britain

Amerang Ltd (Billing)
Commerce Way
Lancing
West Sussex
BN15 8TE

Irvine Engines Ltd
Unit 2
Brunswick Industrial Park
Brunswick Way
New Southgate
London
N11 1JL

Kingston Mouldings
411 Ringwood Road
Parkstone
Poole
Dorset BH12 4LX

Boats and Models
8 Elm Close
Lingwood
Norwich
Norfolk
NR13 4TQ

Modeen Steam Driven Models
PO Box 70
Oldham
Lancs

Stuart Turner Ltd
Henley-on-Thames
Oxon.
RG9 2AD

Lesro Models Ltd
Stony Lane
Christchurch
Dorset
BH23 7LQ

Nylet Ltd
PO Box 7
Fordingbridge
Hants.
SP6 1RQ

Ripmax Ltd
Green Street
Enfield
EN3 7SJ

Prestwich Model Centre
8 Warwick Street
Prestwich
Near Manchester

Dean's Marine
The Old School
Main Street
Farcet
Peterborough

Chart Micro Mold
Chart House
Station Road
East Preston
Littlehampton
West Sussex
BN16 3AG

ABCO UK Ltd
1 Shipton Close
Walshaw Park
Bury
Lancs.
BL8 1QH

Racing Models
1 Melrose Avenue
Whitton
Middlesex

Humbrol Ltd
Marfleet
Hull
HU9 5NE

Plans Service (ASP)
Argus House
Boundary Way
Hemel Hempstead
Herts
HP2 7ST

Sirmar Model Ship Fittings
7 Old Barn Road
Wordsley
Stourbridge
West Midlands
DY8 5XW

H.F.M. Marine
158 Queens Road
Clarendon Park
Leicester
LE2 3FS

C.E. Systems
32 Churchill Crescent
Wickham Market
Suffolk
IP13 0RW

Calder Craft
8 New Street
Meltham
Huddersfield
West Yorkshire
HD7 3NT

United States and Canada

Midwest Products Co. Inc.
400 S. Indiana St.
PO Box 564
Hobart, IN 46342

Mini Marine Racing Equipment
Co.
542 N. Yale
Villa Park, IL 60181

Robbe
180 Township Rd.
Belle Mead, NJ 08502

Dumas Products, Inc.
909-C E. 17th St.
Tuscon, AZ 85719

Octura Models Inc.
7351 N. Hamline Ave.
Skokie, IL 60076

Model Racing Products
12700 NE 124th St. £17
Kirkland, WA 98033

MRC/Tamiya
2500 Woodbridge Ave,
PO Box 267
Edison, NJ 08817

3-D Models
PO Box 972
Port Huron, MI 48060

International Hobbies
1505 Timberline Rd.
Fort Collins, CO 80524

Prather Products
1660 Ravenna Ave.
Wilmington, CA 90744

32nd Parallel
PO Box 804
Pismo Beach, CA 93449

Altech Mktg. Inc.
PO Box 286
Fords, NJ 08863

Dynamic Model Products Inc.
Drawer 'C'
11 Mark St.
Port Jefferson Station, NY 11776

Glen Speckler Radio Models
1709 Benton St.
Bakersfield, CA 93304

DL Products Corp.
PO Box 5
Wheat Ridge, CO 80034

Hartman Fibreglass RC
Box 86, Dept. BG
Argenta, IL 62501

Model Marine Racing Specialties
2440 Andre
Janesville, WI 53543

Model Expo Inc.
23 Just Road
Fairfield, NJ 07006

Norseman Model Marine Co.
518 E. NW Hwy
Mt. Prospect, IL 60056

Radio Controlled Models
4736 N. Milwaukee Ave.
Chicago, IL 60630

SS Boats
3336 S. Summerline Ave.
Orlando, FL 32806

Scale Craft Models Inc.
8735 Shirley Ave.
Northridge, CA 91327

Scale Model Ships Unlimited
54 Rockville Ave.
Staten Island, NY 10314

The Scale Shipyard
5866 Orange Ave. £3
Long Beach, CA 90805

Staubitz of Buffalo
105 Hollybrook Dr.
Williamsville, NY 14221

AG Industries Inc.
1411 4th Ave. £727
Seattle, WA 98101

Index